Come Forward!

I would contend that this book, Come Forward! Bold Enough to Heal and its forerunner, Child Arise, The Courage to Stand, are arguably the most important writings in the life of the Catholic Church in Australia today. Hopefully, some of the lessons learnt in this country will also lead others beyond our shores along the path of healing and reform.

Pat Power, Retired Auxiliary Bishop of Canberra and Goulburn

I am honoured to endorse this book which Jane N. Dowling has written out of her own personal experience, combined with her knowledge of Scriptures. It is an account of her recovery from the trauma of sexual abuse; a story of remarkable courage, gracious spirit, resilience and faith. This is a book by a survivor who has lived through the shame and sorrow of sexual abuse. Come Forward! reveals the wisdom, courage and hope distilled from lived experience of pain and suffering. It is a welcome prayerful resource and a spiritual companion on the journey of life not just for fellow survivors but anyone who is interested in personal healing, growth and transformation. I highly recommend this spiritually enriching book and a unique addition to the narrative of the abuse survivors.

Vincent Long van Nguyen OFM Conv, Bishop of Parramatta

Knowing what it is like to have one's self-worth stolen by a cleric who abused her, Jane N. Dowling finds in the manifold beauty and boldness of Scripture a journey of healing that is grounded in God's unending love. With courage and clarity she shared her story on The Spirit of Things on ABC RN, reaching thousands of people who responded with gratitude. Now with her characteristic sensitivity and a practical method, including art therapy, she makes that journey available to everyone who has doubted themselves and their faith.

Dr Rachael Kohn produced and presented The Spirit of Things on ABC RN, 1997-2018

Jane's "Spiritual Handbook" sheds wonderful and helpful light on an important element of both the damage suffered and, at least for some, the path towards managing life better for those who have suffered church-related sexual abuse.

The spiritual cost for victims/survivors of sexual abuse is rarely if ever addressed by Church protocols, yet it remains for many an essential component in leading a meaningful life. Jane's book provides not only wise insight but a practical strategy for repairing the damage done by church-related abuse and rebuilding the lives of those who have suffered so tragically.

Fr Kevin Dillon AM, "Lifeboat Geelong Foundation"

The title accurately describes a very personal journey of emergence from childhood trauma to new life in Christ. The author gives an honest account of her own hard work of transformation, from being half alive, due to the crippling trauma of abuse, to the discovery of a new personal creation where human flourishing is shaped by new feelings of wellness and self-worth. My own childhood trauma resulted in my mind being closed to creativity and learning, and I can truly recommend this book as a treasure if you dare to imagine life beyond being trapped by memories from childhood.

There is a section on learning personal boundaries; this is an excellent resource for those who have never had the courage to say no to abusive or inappropriate situations. Jane guides the reader in this journey of integration and healing by using Scripture, Visualisations and Art Therapy. God's love is a very personal experience that gives new life to those who have the boldness to ask for that love.

Trish Martin, Theologian and Abuse Survivor

COME FORWARD!

BOLD ENOUGH TO HEAL

A SPIRITUAL HANDBOOK FOR SURVIVORS OF SEXUAL ABUSE
USING SCRIPTURE, VISUALISATION AND ART THERAPY

JANE N. DOWLING

COVENTRY
PRESS

Published in Australia by
Coventry Press
33 Scoresby Road
Bayswater Vic. 3153
Australia

ISBN 9780648566113

Copyright © Jane N. Dowling 2019

All rights reserved. Other than for the purposes and subject to the conditions prescribed under the *Copyright Act*, no part of this publication may be reproduced, stored in a retrieval system, or transmitted in any form or by any means, electronic, mechanical, photocopying, recording or otherwise, without the prior permission of the publisher.

Scripture quotations are from the *New Revised Standard Version Bible*, copyright 1989, Division of Christian Education of the National Council of the Churches of Christ in the United States of America. Used by permission. All rights reserved.

Cataloguing-in-Publication entry is available from the National Library of Australia http://catalogue.nla.gov.au/.

Cover design by Ride High Graphics and Ian James
Text design by FSG (Filmshot Graphics)
Printed in Australia

Contents

Foreword	1
Acknowledgments	5
Introduction	7

Part I Reimagining Self – Transforming our Story in God's Love
    (This part is an invitation to transform our story in God's Love.)

Loved from Dust	24
Breath of Life	29
Hard Places – Sacred Spaces	34
Awesome Miracles	39
Carried not Dumped	46
Divinely Loved	52
Blessed Mountain	59
Something New	64
Succeeding Gracefully	69
Rebuilding the Ruins	73
Dry Bones Revived	77
Life-Giving Reservoirs	83

Part II Coming Forward In Our New Self
    (This part deals with confronting issues that prevent us from moving forward in life.)

Coming Forward - Leaving the hidden life behind	90
Having a Voice	96

Saying "No"	103
Honouring Needs	109
Fracturing Shame	114
Releasing Pain	122
Unwanted Sexual Arousal	130
Self-Worth	140
Healthy Silence	149
Facing Fear	159
Believing without Seeing	166
A New Beginning	179
A blueprint for praying with the Bible	189
Support Services	191

Dedication

For all survivors of sexual abuse
and for those
whose
pain
was
too great.
May they rest forever in peace.

Foreword

WHERE IS THE SPIRIT LEADING the Church today? How is the Catholic Church to regain its credibility in order to proclaim with authenticity the message of Jesus which is so desperately needed in our world today?

The shocking revelations that emerged from the Royal Commission, in some ways, were not unexpected. But the extent of them has been a huge shock to everyone in terms of the numbers involved and the devastating effects on the people concerned.

I would contend that this book, *Come Forward! Bold Enough to Heal* and its forerunner, *Child Arise, The Courage to Stand*, are arguably the most important writings in the life of the Catholic Church in Australia today. Hopefully, some of the lessons learnt in this country will also lead others beyond our shores along the path of healing and reform.

The fact that the author is herself a survivor of child sexual abuse gives her writing a distinct authority. But this does not just flow from her own personal experience but from the sensitivity that has enabled her to understand the damage done to countless others in similar circumstances. She has become a powerful voice for all those on whose behalf she writes.

Jane Dowling steers her readers in the direction of professionals such as counsellors, psychologists and trained trauma specialists. But she also leads her friends into the arms of a loving God, acutely conscious of how their image of God has been distorted by the abuse they have suffered from God's representatives. Right from the outset, in the introduction, Jane gently but clearly states that "God is love". It is a recurring theme of the whole book.

When I became bishop in 1986, I chose as my motto "God is love", arising out of the experience of God's love in twenty-one years as a priest up till then and the blessings of a happy young life before that. I felt humbled to witness Jane Dowling arrive at the same conviction about God's love when in purely human terms she may have been justified in seeing God in a very different light. This is the grace and magic of her writing which gives her readers the pathways to healing, growth and a renewed sense of self-worth.

Her first gift to her readers is to acknowledge without equivocation the huge damage caused by child sexual abuse and its life-long consequences for the people concerned. She is then able to identify various ways in which the suffering continues when the child is unable to share the burden, or, worse, is not believed (and even punished!) in trying to do so. She speaks of "triggers" that bring back to harsh reality the horrors that had lain dormant for a time. Always with great sensitivity and with explicit warnings to proceed with caution, she gently leads her readers to confront the demons that have been thrust upon them.

But they are not left there. In being invited to be bold enough to heal, they are given brilliant strategies to bring about such healing, "Learning to honour our physical, mental, emotional and psychological needs will move us forward on our healing journey."

In a series of exercises, the author encourages prayer, the use of Scripture, visualisation and art therapy with very practical suggestions at the end of each chapter. Most importantly, she strongly recommends journaling, thus enabling her readers to draw on their own wisdom, experiences and moments of grace at later times, especially those in which they feel they have regressed in their journey of healing.

I found her exposition of the various Scripture passages most inspiring, often opening up for me fresh insights into God's Word. I rejoiced in the knowledge that they would have a very special impact on the people for whom this book has been primarily written. "The beauty and absolute gift of listening to God's story of love for us is that our own story is transformed. We begin to see our own story in a new way."

What has emerged from the Royal Commission has not only been the dreadful crimes committed by priests, religious and others in various Church ministries but, all too often, the inadequate (to say the least) response by bishops and other religious people in authority. So much of the initial abuse was compounded by leaders not listening properly and/or seemingly protecting the institution rather than taking steps to redress the great harm done.

Our book gives a moving elucidation of the account of Jesus healing a leper. "What a beautiful role model Jesus is for all religious leaders in our Church if his example is followed. While the Church seeks how to respond to survivors of sexual abuse, the answer is right before us in the person of Jesus, the One it proclaims, who responds to the needs of the poor, the broken and those on the margins of society with love and compassion, healing and restoring them to wholeness and well-being."

It is my prayer that this book will come to the attention of those who have been sexually abused by members of the Catholic Church and that the God of love will lead them further along the journey of love, healing and peace.

I strongly believe that every bishop, priest and religious leader should "come forward" and "be bold enough to heal" by reading this book with a mind and heart open to God and those who have suffered in God's name. So often it is said that we church leaders "don't get it". This book will set us on a journey to do so. The Scriptures tell us: "the truth will set you free".

Pat Power
Retired Auxiliary Bishop of Canberra and Goulburn

Acknowledgments

My heart is warmed and overflowing with gratitude as I remember the people who have been instrumental in the process of bringing this book to you. Your contributions have not only enabled me to complete this book but they have also empowered me to "Come Forward!" on my own journey of healing.

First, I thank God who is not only the "alpha" and "omega" of this book but also the One who has sustained me in the writing process by providing me with the Life and Love needed to work through the inner experiences that I share with you.

I thank my mother and siblings. It has been so painful to watch those I love suffer the inevitable vicarious trauma as a consequence of my decision to come forward and heal.

I thank David Lovell, friend and publisher. David enthusiastically accepted my manuscript submission for *Come Forward* and was eager to publish it; however, David died suddenly in the editing process (26 September 2018). I will always remember David for keenly encouraging me as a writer and for empowering me to have a voice in the public forum. After David's death, I felt his eternal spirit beckoning me to proceed toward publishing – even in death, David's life is still bearing fruit. May you rest in peace forever, David!

I am extremely grateful to all those who gave so generously of their time to read and endorse my book: Fr Kevin Dillon, Rachael Kohn, Bishop Vincent Long and Trish Martin, and also to Bishop Pat Power, who so gladly and vigorously welcomed the invitation to write the Foreword.

Special thanks to Ride High Graphics for the book cover design and for creatively connecting *Come Forward! Bold Enough to Heal* to its forerunner, *Child, Arise! The Courage to Stand*.

Thank you to all those who have provided caring support on my journey: Dr Alison Smith, my psychologist and trauma therapist, who skilfully empowered me to come forward, Nicola and John Ellis who have been there since my decision to come forward to the Royal Commission into Institutional Responses to Child Sexual Abuse, and Bob Munro and Trish Martin from For the Innocents – your empathic listening has been a gift.

I am also enormously thankful to all those who have enriched and supported me on my spiritual journey over the last three decades – transmitting and infusing in me a passion for breaking open the Scriptures in my own life; particularly, Gisella Durante, who has accompanied me spiritually during the last seven years.

I thank my gracious friend Bryan whose, "I am here for you" and capacity to "stay" in the midst of harrowing circumstances have been a personal source of strength, courage and perseverance and a constant reminder of God's faithful love for me.

I am very grateful for all my other beautiful friends (you know who you are) whose listening presence, endowed with understanding and empathy has blessed me on many occasions with a spiritual space of being held and nurtured.

Finally, I would like to extend my heart-felt gratitude to Hugh McGinlay and Coventry Press. It was David Lovell's daughter, Jess, who kindly suggested that I contact Hugh McGinlay with the possibility of moving my manuscript forward towards publication. From the outset, Hugh welcomed my manuscript and reflected enthusiasm for the project. I am very grateful for all the energy that Hugh and Coventry Press have invested in making this book available to you.

Introduction

A short note from the author

THROUGH AN ABUNDANT SUPPLY OF God's grace, I found the courage to come forward. Coming forward has been more than the initial event of breaking my silence and telling someone my truth – I am a survivor of childhood sexual abuse.

Long before I came forward in my outer world, I began a journey of coming forward towards grace and light in my inner world. My journey of coming forward from within is as important, if not more, than coming forward to others. In it, I have discovered an eternal source where I am gifted with everything I need to be bold enough to heal: strength, resilience, courage, confidence, empowerment, gentleness and hope.

For the last three decades of my life, I have been coming forward to others: my psychologist, religious authorities (formerly, I was a member of an international missionary community), my family, my health professionals, the Catholic Church - the institution responsible for the clergy abuse, the Royal Commission into Institutional Responses for Child Sexual Abuse (RCIRCSA), the Police, and as I write this book, I am to come forward as a witness in the Trial of the Accused.

Through my previous book, *Child, Arise! The Courage to Stand. A Spiritual Handbook for Survivors of Sexual Abuse* and this one, I have also come forward.

Each "coming forward" is a story on its own, resembling darkness yet with light, hopelessness yet with hope, fear yet with courage, weakness yet with strength, anger yet with love, powerlessness yet with power and vulnerability yet with resilience.

In this handbook, as I bring you on my own journey of coming forward, I will invite you also to come forward on your own, and hope that you will discover within you the eternal source of all that you need to be bold enough to heal.

The drive behind this spiritual handbook

In November 2012, when Prime Minister Julia Gillard announced a Royal Commission into Institutional Responses to Child Sexual Abuse (RCIRCSA), I don't think anyone could have imagined the magnitude of the issue and how many victims would come forward to tell their stories in both private and public sessions.

At the conclusion of the RCIRCSA (November 2017), 16,953 people who were within the terms of reference had made contact. Of those, 7,981 victims came forward to tell their stories in private sessions, 1,344 victims provided written accounts and 2,562 matters were referred to the police.

In May 2013, I was one of those 7,981 survivors who came forward to tell my story in a private session to the RCIRCSA. By coming forward, I know first-hand the re-traumatisation that is experienced. Yet, even for those survivors who choose not to come forward, re-traumatisation occurred due to the constant media coverage that was given to the RCIRCSA.

As a survivor witnessing the RCIRCSA calling individuals and institutions to be responsible and accountable for their past actions, it is emotionally very stirring. While it has been necessary to expose a truth long covered up and while it has delivered victims and their families a sense of justice, it has also opened up very deep wounds in survivors, exposing raw emotions.

As the work of the RCIRCSA concludes, the work of survivors to heal their wounds will be life-long, not only for those who came forward to tell their stories but also those who chose not to and are hurting alone and silently.

During the RCIRCSA, I have been particularly aware of the deep spiritual wounds that may have been re-opened for survivors of clergy child sexual abuse; spiritual wounds that have left many estranged from the faith they knew as an innocent child before it was tragically assaulted and left others holding on to their faith by a very thin thread. Presently there is an urgent need for healing resources that address the spiritual impacts of child sexual abuse, particularly for those who have experienced sexual abuse by a member of the clergy.

As a survivor of clergy child sexual abuse, I have spent decades attending to my own spiritual wounds. These wounds ran so deep that I thought at one stage, it is impossible to ever heal the spiritual dimension of my life. Grace disproved me and, through an abundance of it, I began to experience the powerful, transforming and healing love of God restoring what had been grossly severed. As the spiritual dimension began to heal, meaning and purpose returned to my life. This emphasised for me how important it is for survivors to gradually experience spiritual healing, for if this dimension remains broken, survivors may struggle endlessly to find meaning and purpose for their life. This created in me a deeper restlessness to make my own experience of healing the spiritual impacts available to other survivors.

In this book, *Come Forward! Bold Enough to Heal. A Spiritual Handbook for Survivors of Sexual Abuse using Scripture, Visualisation and Art Therapy*, as well as my previous book, *Child, Arise! The Courage to Stand. A Spiritual Handbook for Survivors of Sexual Abuse*, I do this in written form as I speak 'survivor to survivor', and walk with survivors, accompanying each to have their own experience of God's healing love.

During the development of this second handbook, I have been engaged in some enormously painful events around my past trauma, but as with my first handbook, these events became the perfect ground for my writing and provided me with the raw material that was also to become God's working field and the place where God would meet me and speak to me through the Scriptures, and the place from which I would then speak to you and communicate what is contained in this handbook.

While the process of writing this book has come at a cost – physically, emotionally and psychologically– I have been gifted with an even more outstanding experience – one of God's transforming and healing love at work in my life through the Scriptures. This has been empowering and given me the boldness to keep coming forward on my healing journey. So with these very same wishes for you, I have been driven to complete this book.

My hopes for this book

I truly hope that this book will follow as a continuum to my first handbook, *Child, Arise! The Courage to Stand. A Spiritual Handbook for Survivors of Sexual Abuse* and that it will be a practical spiritual handbook for survivors of sexual abuse to assist in the journey of integration and healing through Scripture, visualisation and art therapy.

The added component of art therapy in this second handbook is intentional. Often, survivors express an inability to articulate their traumatic experiences. The invitation to gently explore the Scripture through art therapy and creative expression will facilitate survivors who find it difficult to articulate their inner world to form a language of words. At the conclusion of this handbook, the reader will end up with an art journal that visually captures their own healing journey. I hope that survivors may experience how Scripture combined with art therapy is a powerful tool that empowers them to put words to their traumatic experiences.

This handbook is not meant to replace other psychological therapies or supports that are part of the survivor's network. On the contrary, it may be used in conjunction with these and found to be complementary. For example, if a survivor feels comfortable enough, the art journal is something that may be brought to a counselling or psychological session, or shown to someone who is supporting them to assist in articulating their experiences.

I hope that this handbook will also benefit family and friends of survivors, as well as members of the clergy and religious, to gain deeper insight into the life-long impacts and effects of child sexual abuse and the journey that is implied for healing. You too may find yourself doing the walk as you work through the Scripture reflections offered in this handbook.

I am also hoping that this handbook will be a useful resource for those who are pastorally and spiritually accompanying survivors of sexual abuse and that the content and structure of this handbook may be useful for the formation of facilitated spiritual support groups for survivors that are made as safe as possible with professional support[1].

Perhaps some who pick up this handbook have not been exposed to faith, and others abandoned their faith very early on due to the spiritual impacts of

---

1 I highlight the word "professional". It is important for survivors to feel safe and well supported within established groups through the presence of professionals, that is, counsellors, psychologists, trained trauma specialists.

Introduction

child sexual abuse but now experience a gentle stirring to return to it. Finally, there may be those holding on to their faith by a very thin thread who need it to become a life-saving rope and stronghold for their life. No matter where each one is on their healing journey or journey of faith, my hope is that the reflections in this book will resonate with you and that you will be able to engage with them positively and be empowered by them in your daily living. More than anything, I hope that through this handbook you will discover that you are never alone because the God who created you and gifted you with the breath of Life, is with you always, in all the highs and lows of your healing journey.

For survivors who have been sexually abused by a member of the clergy and experience how their faith in God has been gravely impacted, I hope you will find this handbook helpful. One of the most painful impacts of clergy sexual abuse is how it horribly distorts the image of God. Characteristics that belonged to the survivor's perpetrator become enmeshed with the survivor's image of God, meaning that if the perpetrator was violent, angry and someone to be feared, then the survivor's image of God will be the same. For this reason, survivors will often describe God as someone who is cold, uncaring, tough, punishing, and angry; and someone who doesn't care.

I hope that as you work through the reflections in this handbook, you will begin to identify your own false and distorted images of God and discover a means of working through them for the future. My hope is that over time, these false images will gradually dissolve, enabling you to hear a story even bigger than your own; the story of God's great love for your life - a God who is close, familiar and, most of all loving – because this is who God is – Love[2].

As you do this, I hope you will come to a deeper appreciation of the healing and integrative power that God's Word in the Scriptures offers us when it is listened to, believed and practised in life, and how, through it, God will do new and amazing things in your life so that you are surprised again and again.

My final hope is that as you come to the end of this handbook, you have been empowered to come forward and are bold enough to keep healing, knowing that you never walk alone but in the powerful presence of an all loving and tender God.

---

2 1 John 4:8

As you come forward both from within and without, may you savour and enjoy the gift of God who is the summer of our story; the One who brings a sunshine of strong light, rays of warmth, abundance of new growth and opening up of new life, and refreshing summer breezes of hope.

Getting the most out of this handbook

This book is meant to be a practical spiritual handbook that survivors of sexual abuse can refer to time and time again as a tool for their own personal healing. By revisiting chapters, you will be able to gauge where you were at previously when you reflected on the particular issue, expressed visually through your art journal, and where you are at present. This enables you to appreciate the journey forward you are doing.

This book is not meant to be used as a study guide of the Bible – which is why the scriptural reflections contained in it do not attempt to explain fully the historical, religious or cultural context behind the specific Scripture readings. Instead, it is meant to be a practical tool that can be used for prayerful reflection on Scripture so that practical applications can be made and later practised. To achieve this, you will notice that the scriptural reflections in parts I and II highlight issues that are significant for survivors (yet may also resonate with non-survivors) and provide an explanation of the theological relevance for survivors of sexual abuse. It is important to keep this in mind when you are reading these reflections.

Experiencing the Scripture through Art

Throughout this book, you will be invited to creatively express your own journey of healing through Scripture, visualisation and art therapy. To engage with the contents of this book, you don't need to be an artist and know how to draw perfect figures or objects. The invitation to explore the Scripture and your own journey through art is more about creatively connecting to your inner world and expressing your own feelings and thoughts. By the end of this book, you may decide that you would like to continue creatively expressing yourself through art as part of your spiritual practice since it is not only a powerful means of letting go but also of opening ourselves up to new things. Many of the issues that survivors deal with are challenging and stressful, and involve intense emotions. Creatively expressing yourself through art can relieve some of the stress and dissipate the intensity of your emotions; it may even surprise you with answers of how to come forward on your journey. As Thomas Merton said, "Art enables us to find ourselves and lose ourselves at the same time".

So before you proceed to Part I of this handbook, I would suggest having an A3 size art book, along with either some colour crayons, water paints, pencils, textas, chalks or whatever you prefer to work with so that you can create your own Art Journal.

Creating a language through journaling

To complement this, in Part II, you will also be invited to keep a writing Journal where can give written expression to your art and healing journey. For survivors who do not have a language around their trauma and who find it difficult to articulate inner feelings and thoughts, you may find this particularly helpful. It is helpful to have written accounts of our prayerful encounters with God and the insights of our journey to refer back to in the future, particularly when we are immersed in darkness and lack hope. Revisiting our writing journal can rekindle our courage and perseverance. It is also a very tangible way of recalling God's presence in our life and the work of grace that God is achieving in our personal story.

A guide to the reflections in this handbook

This uniqueness of this handbook lies in the applications of the scriptural readings used in Parts I and II alike, that are specifically applied to the context of survivors of child sexual abuse (although non-survivors may also find them beneficial). The goal is to assist survivors to experience that the Word God speaks through Scriptures is relevant to survivors and in it we can experience the closeness and healing love of God.

It is important to say that, out of sensitivity to those who have been wounded by men, and for greater inclusiveness, I have tried to refrain from using masculine terms to refer to God, even though God is mostly referred to in masculine terms throughout the Bible. When I do use masculine terms, it is either because I am being faithful to the scriptural text I am referring to or because it is important in the context of that sentence. While God is also referred to using feminine images in the Bible, particularly that of the mother, it is important to keep in mind that God is beyond human gender, whether male or female – God is God. This is something to remember whenever 'he', or 'him', or 'his' is used.

Part I: Reimagining Self – Transforming our Story in God's Love

Often, we are not aware that the entirety of our story is lived within a much bigger story – God's story of love for us. These two stories are intimately connected; for as our story unfolds, so too does God's story of love for us. Even though we feel that God is far away at times, the reality is that God is closer than we can imagine for as the Scriptures remind us, "in him we live, move and have our being".[3] The unchangeable truth is that our story is being held and anchored in God's own story of love for us, no matter how broken or hopeless our story is.

Sadly, we can go through the whole of our life without ever having listened to God's story of unending love for us – how God loved us into life and promises to do so for eternity, how God fought for us when no one else did, how God cared for us when it seemed that no one cared for us, how God held our pain when no one else could, how God cried with us when we poured out tears, how God carried us when we were tired, how God provided for us when we were in need. At the end of our life, as our story comes to a close, perhaps it does so without ever having known the immensity of God's love for us.

I am aware that for survivors of clergy child sexual abuse, who were brought up with faith, opening our heart to listen to God's story of personal love for us is challenging. Clergy sexual abuse has a direct spiritual impact on

---
3 Acts 17:28

Introduction

the survivor's relationship with God because of the association that the clergy perpetrator, referred to as "Father" in the Catholic Church, was supposed to represent God. What happened then in the child's mind was inevitable; for the child being abused, the clergy perpetrator is equal to God; therefore, the concluding equation is that the characteristics of the clergy perpetrator are equal to the characteristics of God. As a survivor grows into adulthood, even though a relationship with God may be desired, it seems too hard because their heart is full of barriers, walls and blocks as a consequence of the trauma.

I too have had to walk a very long journey of healing these spiritual impacts. In my first book, I describe how my turning point came at a time when I had hit rock bottom. My state was unbearable and I was suicidal.

Thankfully, grace intervened. I felt prompted to open a Bible that my mother kept on my bedside table. The words I opened up to that jumped out at me were from the book of the Prophet Isaiah (43:1)

> But now thus says the LORD,
> he who created you, O Jacob,
> he who formed you, O Israel:
> Do not fear, for I have redeemed you;
> I have called you by name, you are mine.

These words went to the core of my being, deep into my inner chaos and darkness. I felt like I had been seen and found. I was known to someone who knew I felt afraid and beckoned me not to be, and this someone called me by name and told me 'you are mine' offering me a sense of belonging.

There are so many things that I cannot remember as a result of my childhood trauma but my memory of the day I read these words from Scripture is crystal clear. I was awe-struck because the words felt so absolutely personal. There was something wonderfully powerful about them. Although they were written down on paper, I knew in my heart that the heartbeat of the Sacred Presence was behind them. I knew that the 'someone' saying these words to me was God.

It was a watershed moment and one that was life-changing for me. I experienced that through this Scripture reading, God had come to search for me and God found me in my very chaotic and dark world. Even though it was very subtle at the time, these words caused something to shift within me so that I felt different after reading these words. It was like a door of light and hope had been opened through the Scriptures and these were now stretching into my darkness. It's no wonder that the words of the song, "Amazing grace, how sweet the sound, that saved a wretch like me", really ring home for me.

This experience initiated me into listening to God's story of personal love for me. It's a story that is intriguing, mystifying, holds me in suspense. At times, it's overwhelming, it's captivating, it's always new and truly never boring.

This is the gift that I would like to gently introduce the reader to in Part I – Listening to God's story of personal love for you through the Scriptures - so that you too can discover how God looks at your life with love, how God thinks about you with love, how God feels towards you, and, most importantly, how God is walking with you in life.

The beauty and absolute gift of listening to God's story of love for us, is that our own story is transformed. We begin to see our own story in a new way. We begin to think and feel differently about our story, we begin to act and behave differently, and our attitudes shift and change as we experience in our body and spirit the almighty, "Ephphatha[4] (meaning be opened)", the word Jesus spoke to the deaf and mute man in Mark's gospel whose hearing and speech impediment was removed – a beautiful example of a story transformed in the story of God's personal love. It is the miracle that takes place in us as we engage with God's Word through the Scriptures.

This is the journey we will begin in Part I as I lead you gently through the Scriptures. The reflections in Part I refer to readings from the Old Testament (also referred to as the Hebrew Scriptures), beginning with the book of Genesis. Too often, God in the Hebrew Scriptures is described as being angry, punishing, cold, far away and uncaring – an image that resonates with survivors of sexual abuse. Hopefully, the reflections in Part I will lead you to experience that a God of Love is very palpable in the Hebrew Scriptures.

The Scripture readings that I have chosen are very visual readings so that we can engage our imaginations in the prayerful reflection and express it creatively

---

4   Mark 7:34

through art. I hope that these reflections create in you surprise, awe, wonder, astonishment and fill you with grace.

It is important to do each one of the Scripture reflections in Part I in the order in which they appear because each reflection acts as a stepping stone for the one that follows it.

I would suggest doing one reflection per day or you may choose to spend several days on a single reflection.

Experiencing the Scripture through Art

Keep in mind that this is a spiritual handbook for healing and it's not intended to be read as you would read a novel. Working through this handbook is about honouring and taking ownership of your own healing process. This means giving yourself the appropriate time and space to ponder the truth and the story of love that God is communicating to you through the particular chapter.

The intention of experiencing Scripture through Art not only enables you to creatively express what God is communicating to you through the Scriptures but it also helps to slow down the pace and give you time to process. Experiencing the Scripture through Art is about creating a prayerful space for pondering, questioning, exploring deeper questions, and searching for the truth in a more relaxed way. It is gentle way of slowly and carefully undoing our false images of God.

So, as you move through Part I, I hope you enjoy listening to the story of God's great love for you – a story that began even before you were being intricately woven in your mother's womb[5] and a story that continues throughout your life until you reach old age and your hairs are grey[6] and then continues into eternity. It is a powerful and moving story of love, a love that has suffered for us and with us, a love that has put everything on the line for us, a love that believes in us. May you taste and savour God's story of love for your life and as you listen to it, may you experience the grace and power it has to transform your own story in ways that you would never imagine.

---

5   Psalm 139:13-16
6   Isaiah 46:4

Part II: Coming Forward in our New Self

This part invites the reader to come forward in the inner and outer healing journey of dealing with the impacts and effects of sexual abuse.

Survivors experience the impacts and effects of sexual abuse in their life on a daily basis. While there are effects and issues that are common to adult survivors, the prevalence of the issue in each survivor may vary. What may be a debilitating issue in one survivor may be to a lesser degree in another. This doesn't mean that one survivor has suffered a lesser trauma than the other but it suggests that the context surrounding each person's trauma, and their responses to it may have been very different. This emphasises that each survivor's story is unique!

The reflections contained in Part II are some of the issues I was facing on my journey while writing this book. It has been impossible for me to address all the issues that survivors of sexual abuse are faced with since the trauma affects us in multiple ways and aspects of our life.

You may choose to work through the reflections of Part II in the order they appear or you may choose to do a specific reflection that responds to an issue you are dealing with on a particular day. Choose a time that works best for you, when you know that you will not be interrupted by other things. Take as much time as you need to work through each reflection even if it means coming back to it over a couple of days. Move onto the next reflection when you feel ready to.

It is quite normal, as we go deeper into the layers of our trauma, that down the track, certain issues re-surface in which case you may choose to re-visit and re-work the reflection. The beauty of reflecting on God's Word is that, although the Scripture we read on a given day may be the same as one we have read in the past, what we listen to will be different because our circumstances and the context in which we are listening to the words from Scripture are different. There will always be something in our experience today that is new from our experience of yesterday.

Each reflection has the following structure:

The issue is named

A specific issue is outlined. At times, I refer to how I was experiencing the issue in my life at the given time.

Scripture reading

A reflection on a specific Scripture reading is offered, highlighting the issue being addressed. The explanation does not attempt to address the cultural, historical or religious context of the Scripture reading but it attempts to explain the spiritual relevance, referring to the issue in a way that is practical and applicable for survivors. This enables survivors to experience how God's Word can empower them to come forward and to move through the issues and effects of sexual abuse that are experienced on a daily basis.

Experiencing the Scripture through Prayer, Visualisation and Art

In this section, you will be invited to experience the Scripture first through prayer.

Prayer is a relationship with God that is developed through dialogue: God talks to us and we listen to God. Thinking about God with our mind, which is what we do when we meditate or reflect on Scripture, is very different to relating to God. Relating to God implies our whole being: body, mind, heart, spirit and emotions. Hopefully, this section will assist in developing a relationship with God.

This section includes steps that are a guide to facilitate your own personal time of praying with the Scripture. To enhance your prayer experience, you will also be invited to creatively express your personal prayer experience through art. Remember, you don't need to be an artist - it's not about drawing perfect figures or objects but rather creatively expressing how the Scripture reading is speaking to you. The guided steps will assist you to do this and by following them, you will gradually learn how to let the words of Scripture speak to your own life and the issues you are dealing with on your journey.

Hopefully, you will also experience how taking time to express our prayer through art also assists us to deepen our listening to the Scriptures and apply them personally to our lives. It is always surprising to experience how the finished work of art that we have created expresses more than we intended as we were drawing. For this reason, you will be invited to spend time reflecting on your own art work at the end of each section.

Our faith is strengthened when we practise what we experience in prayer. The final steps of the guided activity will invite you to arrive at a practical resolution. Practising does not mean that we are always going to get it right! Don't be discouraged if you find you fail often. Like any gift or talent that we attempt to develop, it needs practice. Practice is not about getting it right all the time. Often, we may fail but the clue is humility and giving it another go. It is the same when it comes to practising our faith. The more we practise what we listen to and understand in prayer, the more empowered we are to come forward on our healing journey.

By the time you reach the end of the book, by working through the steps in this section, you will have developed a method for experiencing the Scriptures through prayer, visualisation and art therapy that you can continue to use in the future even with other Scriptures not mentioned in this book. For you own benefit, you will have created an art journal that visually captures your own healing journey of coming forward and demonstrates your boldness to heal. You may find it encouraging to re-visit your art journal in the future as a reminder of the healing that is already unfolding in your life. You may find it helpful to refer to your art journal in your psychological/counselling sessions.

In the Appendix, you will find a blueprint for Praying with the Scriptures that you may find useful in the future.

The Scripture Experienced in my Life / My Experience of Scripture through Art

In this section, I either give a brief and personal account of how God invited me to practise and live out the words of Scripture in my daily life, or share my experience of the Scripture through Art.

Introduction

Your experience of Scripture through prayer, visualisation and art

In this section, you are invited to journal about your own experience of the Scripture through prayer and art. Hopefully, this will assist you in creating and developing a language around your own healing journey and that this can benefit you when it comes to sharing your story in the appropriate contexts and with the appropriate people.

Your journal will tell the story of your boldness to come forward from tragedy and heal. It will be a testament of how God's love is working in you and transforming your own personal story.

Be attuned to this new moment in your life.

PART I

Reimagining Self - Transforming our Story in God's Love

(This part is an invitation to transform our story in God's Love.)

Loved from Dust

Then the Lord God formed man from the dust of the ground.[7]

Genesis 2:7

THE HUMBLE ORIGINS OF HUMANKIND are reflected so graphically in the Second Creation Story of the Scriptures (Genesis 2:4b-25). We can imagine God physically moulding humankind "from the dust of the ground" somewhat like a potter forming clay. It's a very different image from the First Creation Story where humankind is created in the divine image of God (Genesis 1:26)! Common to both Creation Stories is the tender love of the Creator who wills humankind into being.

Perhaps the Second Creation Story resonates with survivors of sexual abuse more than the first because of the "earthy" images and language. It speaks of the "dust of the ground" which conjures up images of filth, dirt, scum and rubbish. These images often arise for survivors of sexual abuse and we translate them into words by telling others we feel like "dirt", "crap", "rubbish", or "shit" (pardon the expression)!

For survivors, these feelings may give rise to different ways of behaving. I have spoken to some who have the need to shower several times a day in the hope of washing away all the "dirt" of the sexual abuse and then there are some

---

[7] In many English translations of Genesis 2, the first human is simply called "man". This "man" is understood by most people as referring to a male human rather than to a generic human. However, in the Hebrew text, the first "man" is not specifically referred to as a male human (*ish*) until after the "operation" mentioned in Genesis 2:21-22 when a part, or side, is taken out of him. In Genesis 1:27 it says that "God created humankind (ha'adam) in his own image, in the image of God he created him; male and female he created them." In Genesis 2, the first human is fairly consistently referred to as ha'adam (הָאָדָם), especially before the "operation". (Barbara Aland and the Nestle-Aland Greek NT http://newlife.id.au/equality-and-gender-issues/human-man-woman-genesis-2/)

who go to the other extreme and who won't wash themselves because they say, "I feel like shit anyway!"

I met one young lady who was admitted to hospital after being sexually abused. She was experiencing post-traumatic stress disorder (PTSD). She told me that she didn't want to eat or drink anything because her mouth felt so dirty and contaminated. Being a survivor myself, I understood this but unfortunately the doctors and nursing staff didn't and she was put into the "non-compliant" category. I advocated for the young lady with the medical and nursing staff to help them understand what was happening to the young lady.

The sense of feeling "dirty" can be manifested in the life of survivors in multiple ways. It even invades experiences that one would normally refer to as "beautiful". Like recently, I was going through something difficult and a good friend of mine put their hand on mine as a way of gently saying, "I am here for you!" I knew that this was the intention in my mind but sadly, through the gesture of touch, my body was remembering other experiences and at that moment, instead of feeling "how beautiful", I felt "dirty", so dirty that I had to get up and wash my hands.

Unfortunately, the most beautiful gestures of friendship and intimacy that normally lead a person to experience joy and celebration can often leave survivors of sexual abuse feeling filthy, even though these gestures are being experienced in a context of authentic friendship and very different to the context of the sexual abuse.

For years, I struggled to come to terms with these feeling of "dirtiness" that would repeatedly arise within me. Initially, I attempted to push down these feelings and pretend that they weren't there. This didn't work. One day, I tried something different. I tried not to panic when the feeling of "dirtiness" arose and instead of pushing the feelings back down again, I tried to acknowledge I was feeling "plain dirty". The feeling was so intense that I felt every part of me was covered in dust and scum. I felt so dirty that I thought, "not even the longest shower in the world could make me clean".

As I gave myself permission to feel the "dirtiness" that my body was remembering from the sexual abuse, deep questions began to surface in me. Can anyone possibly love me when I feel so dirty? Is it possible that this sense of feeling "dirty" and like "scum of the earth" could ever be transformed into something beautiful?

The search for profound answers to these questions led me to the Second Creation Story.

The "dust of the ground", in other words, the "dirt" is not counted as useless or worthless for God. When God is creating the world, God doesn't try to get rid of all the dirt and clean it up. God does something beyond imagination! God looks at the "dust" and "dirt" with great love and sees a great possibility to create something totally new out of it. God tenderly picks up the "dust of the ground" and creatively forms a masterpiece – humankind. God is so pleased with this new creation – humankind - that God claims it to be "very good"[8].

In the same way, God doesn't reject us or count us as worthless when we feel like "shit" or "dirt" or "rubbish". God won't discard us. On the contrary, it's precisely when we feel this way that God desires to love us deeply and invites us to believe that in the same way God worked tenderly with the dust off the ground in the Creation Story and formed something "very good" out of it, that God will do the same for us.

If we can open ourselves, even slightly, to this new possibility and allow God to love us when we feel dirty, it may be the beginning of something "very good" that is beyond our imagination taking place within us.

As we allow God to work with our "dirt", we may even begin to experience that the things that once caused us to feel dirty like holding a hand, or a kiss from a friend, no longer do because God has worked with our feelings of "dirt" and reshaped them into something new so that these gestures no longer provoke feelings of "dirtiness" associated with the sexual abuse but rather "very good" feelings of love, friendship and support.

---

8 Genesis 1:31

Experiencing the Scripture through Art
(Suggested materials: an A4 or A3 drawing book, crayons, paints or coloured pencils)

1. On a fresh page, you may like to put the title: "Loved from Dust".
2. Divide the page in half by drawing a line down it.
3. On the left side, using the colours of your choice:
    i) Draw a pair of hands. These hands represent God's hands.
    ii) Inside the pair of hands, draw either some dirty earth or dust particles. (Again use the colour of your choice.) This dirty earth and dust particles represent the things and experiences that make you feel dirty. This will be different for each survivor. I have shared that someone holding my hand or greeting me with a kiss can do this for me. For others it may be other gestures, being in certain places, certain items of clothing...
    iii) In another colour, you may like to write/name what the dust is for you.
4. As you look at what you have drawn, what does it say to you that you have not realised before? (For example, looking at my drawing I understood that God doesn't reject me when I feel dirty but is holding me with love). You may want to write this in a few words under what you have drawn.
5. Perhaps you may find it helpful to keep coming back to this picture as you journey forward to remember what you have realised.
6. On the right side, using the colours of your choice:
    i) Again, draw a pair of hands that represent God's hands working with your dust.
    ii) Take a moment to visualise God working with the dust and dirt that you have named on the left hand side. Visualise how God is looking at your "dust" with

great possibilities. Visualise God picking up your dust and creating something new with it. What do you visualise emerging?

    iii) Take some time now to draw what you have visualised.

7. As you look at what you have drawn, what does your picture communicate to you? For example, it may include:
    i) God can create something new and good from my experiences of feeling dirty
    ii) I am loved by God even when I feel dirty
    iii) My feeling like "dirt" and "crap" is useful and worthy for God
    iv) I can be different
8. You may like to write this in a few words under what you have drawn.

In the future, whenever you feel like "crap" or "dirt" or "shit" or "rubbish", you may like to come back to this picture and let God remind you of how you have been loved and created from the "dust of the ground" and how God desires to keep loving you even when you feel like rubbish, and recreating you beyond imagination!

Breath of Life[9]

...And God breathed into his nostrils the breath of Life; and the man became a living being.[10]

Genesis 2:7

NOT ONLY DID GOD LOVINGLY mould us from dust but God then gave humankind Life. God did not want us to remain lifeless human beings. God loved humankind so much that God willed us to become a "living being".

The God we know in the Bible is a God of Life, not a God of death. From the beginning of our Creation, God's greatest desire for us was to be living beings who are fully alive, not lifeless beings who feel dead from within.[11] So intense was God's will for us that God breathed into us the breath of Life and we too became a living being. From the very breath of God we have come to have Life. Our very first breath was a gift of Life from God and each breath we breathe is a gift of Life from God. God's breath continues to keep us alive.

It is fascinating to ponder about the very first "breath of Life" that God breathed into us. It is the same "breath" that existed at the beginning of time and through which all living things came to be[12]. In receiving God's breath of Life, we have received God's very own Life[13].

---

9 For some survivors, the imagery in this Scripture may trigger flashbacks which will be addressed later in this chapter. A "flashback" is the re-emergence of a traumatic memory as a vivid recollection of sounds, images and sensations associated with the trauma. For the person having the flashback, they typically feel as if they are re-living the event.
10 See footnote 7
11 In the Gospel of John 10:10 Jesus reveals that his coming is to fulfil God's greatest desire for us, "I came that they may have life, and have it abundantly."
12 John 1:3, Colossians 1:16
13 1 John 1:2

What does it mean that God has breathed into us God's very own Life? It means that we have God's very own nature pumping through our body. God's nature is best summed up in the First Letter of John who tells us that "God is Love"[14] and in Paul's First Letter to the Corinthians, he describes the characteristics of God's love, "Love is patient and kind; love is not jealous or boastful; it is not arrogant or rude. Love does not insist on its own way; it is not irritable or resentful; it does not rejoice at wrong, but rejoices in the right. Love bears all things, believes all things, hopes all things, endures all things. Love never ends."[15]

So if we imagine the very first "breath of Life" that God breathed into us, we may imagine God breathing God's own Life in us – Love – that is, all the characteristics mentioned above, as well as all the other characteristics of God's Love that Paul fails to mention but we know to be God's love like: compassion, generosity, joy, strength, and gentleness, just to name a few.

I am aware that for some survivors of sexual abuse, the phrase "breath of life" may trigger some traumatic memories, depending on the individual's context of sexual abuse. If attempts were made to ever suffocate the survivor, or simply a survivor's breath was stifled in one way or another, then the survivor may experience recurrent memories through flashbacks or night terrors. If you are like me, you may wake up often in the night gasping for breath with a sense that you are choking or have stopped breathing or can't get breath in. Being able to connect these events to our past experiences with the support and help of a good therapist is very helpful.

I have shared with survivors who have articulated that one of the spiritual impacts of the sexual abuse is feeling as if life from within and without has been stifled and suffocated. In a sense, it is as though the crime of our perpetrator(s) has taken our "breath" away.

---

14   1 John 4:8
15   1 Corinthians 13:4-8a

It is not uncommon for survivors to often ask themselves, "What if this didn't happen to me? How would my life be now? Would I be more fruitful in making a contribution to the world? Would I respond differently to situations?"

We have been robbed of life in so many ways: robbed of time, robbed of good physical, mental, psychological, emotional and spiritual health; consequently robbed of good and healthy relationships, robbed of the pleasure of experiencing authentic love, robbed of career possibilities, robbed of good financial prospects, robbed of a faith/relationship with God. All of this can leave us feeling spiritually lifeless and breathless.

Since coming forward for my Private Hearing Session with the Royal Commission for Institutional Responses to Child Sexual Abuse (RCIRCSA) in May 2013 and making the decision to pursue prosecution in August 2013, I have often found myself reflecting on how much of all the above I, and all survivors who decide to pursue prosecution, have been robbed of as we pursue the course of justice. Simply reflecting on the time I have felt robbed of in the process is astounding: time spent in psychological sessions, time to attend doctor's appointments and medical examinations, time working with detectives, time on the telephone and travelling by public transport to follow up issues, time to meet with significant people like lawyers, time required away from work and studies, time away from family and friends...

If I would add up all the hours I have spent on the prosecution case since 2013, it would not alarm me that I have spent more time dealing with these matters than I have working and studying. As I write this, I am waiting to bear witness in my perpetrator's trial and I am aware that this will come with a personal cost which will require dealing with the effects and impacts of re-traumatisation, yet again robbing me of more time in the future. However, this is the cost of justice.

Nonetheless, in this state of lifelessness, God breathes into us the breath of Life, that is, God's very own Life of Love.

You may find the following activity helps you to experience how God does this.

Experiencing the Scripture through visualisation and art
(Suggested materials: an A4 or A3 drawing book, crayons, paints or coloured pencils)

1. You may like to title the page: "Breath of Life".
2. Divide your page in half by drawing a line down it.
3. On the left side:
    i) Try to draw what feeling breathless, stifled or suffocated looks like for you.
    ii) Reflect on the things in your life that make you feel this way. You may like to write the name of these things around your drawing.
4. Take some time to reflect on God's breath being the very nature of God who is Love (1 John 4:8).
5. Try to visualise God breathing the "breath of Life"[16] into you, that is the very essence of who God is – Love – with all its characteristics.
    i) Take your time to visualise God's breath of Life entering your whole being and permeating every organ, tissue, muscle, bone, fibre, cell.
    ii) Visualise God breathing patience in you and permeating your whole body. Likewise, take your

---

16 Being touched in an intimate way, as with a kiss, or imagining God breathing breath into us, may stir up terrifying memories associated with the perpetrator. I will leave it to the survivor to discern if they would like to continue with this activity or not. In the case that you would like to continue but experience painful memories or flashbacks, you may find that working through the following steps is helpful to overcome some of the spiritual impacts that sexual abuse has had on your relationship with God: 1. Was there a particular thought that came to your mind or did you experience a flashback? 2. As this came to you, what were you feeling? (Anxiety, fear, terror…) 3. Try to identify who these thoughts, flashbacks, or feelings refer to? (For example, your perpetrator) 4. Once you have identified who your responses refer to, try to be aware that now you are in the presence of God who is Love and not in the presence of your perpetrator. Some self-talk may be helpful, for example, "I am safe! I am not with my perpetrator. I am with God who is Love. God is not like my perpetrator and not my perpetrator. God and my perpetrator are very different." 5. You may want to tell God how you feel as you try to imagine God breathing the "breath of Life" in you (For example, God I am so scared as I think about letting you breath your breath of Life in me!). 6. Try to silence all the noises in your heart and let God assure you "I am God and not your perpetrator!" 7. If you feel calm enough, you may want to proceed with the activity.

time to visualise God breathing kindness into you (pause), then truth (pause), then joy (pause), and so on.

6. As you visualise God's breath of Life entering you, what happens to the things that are suffocating or stifling Life within you? (Before doing this activity, I felt my life was being stifled by needing to attend another appointment today around the prosecution case. I didn't have energy but as God breathed his life into me, I felt renewed energy).
7. How do you feel as you visualise this? (I felt lighter, more positive and motivated.)
8. On the right hand side:
    i) Try to draw what the things that stifle and suffocate you look like as God breathes Life into them?
9. As you look at the picture what does it communicate to you about:
    i) Image of God (For example: God wants me to have Life not death, God cares for me when I am lifeless, God nurtures me with Life, God sustains my Life, God is energy). You may like to write that in a few words around your picture.
10. How do you feel as you look at your drawing? (You may want to write this somewhere around your picture.)

Try to keep this image in your mind and heart as you go forward today. Whenever you experience that your spiritual life is being stifled or suffocated, it may be helpful for you to come back to this Scripture. Read it slowly, take time to ponder it and then go back to your picture and recall what God has communicated to you. Or you may simply want to visualise anew God breathing fresh Life into you and draw what that looks like for you.

Hard Places – Sacred Spaces

"Jacob left Beer-sheba and went toward Haran. He came to a certain place and stayed there for the night, because the sun had set. **Taking one of the stones of the place, he put it under his head and lay down in that place.** *And he dreamed that there was a ladder set up on the earth, the top of it reaching to the heaven; and the angels of God were ascending and descending on it. And the Lord stood beside him and said....* "*Know that I am with you and will keep you wherever you go, and will bring you back to the land; for I will not leave you until I have done what I have promised you." Then Jacob woke from his sleep and said,* "**Surely the Lord is in this place – and I did not know it!**"

Genesis 28:10-13a; 15-16

THIS STORY PORTRAYS JACOB'S FIRST encounter with God. Jacob is the son of Isaac and the younger brother of Esau. Before Isaac dies, Jacob deceives him into receiving his Patriarchal blessing, a blessing that rightfully belonged to his older brother Esau. When Esau finds out, he is furious with his brother Jacob and he plans to kill him. Jacob's mother, Rebekah, beckons Jacob to flee for his safety and again, he receives his father's blessing.

Through this story, we get a glimpse of Jacob at a point on his journey where he feels most vulnerable as he flees his home at Beer-sheba and sets out to a foreign land. Jacob comes to a "certain place" and he "stays there for the night because the sun had set".

When Jacob arrives physically to this "certain place", we can imagine that spiritually it is also a very hard "place" for Jacob to be where the comfort of light has been dispelled by darkness – a darkness that emphasises his feelings of fear, anxiety, insecurity, uncertainty, loss and pain, as he leaves all that he is familiar with and journeys towards the unknown. It is at this "certain place" that Jacob chooses to "stay" for the night.

Jacob lays his head on one of the "stones of the place". The "stone" signifies a sacred space (Genesis 28:22) and as he sleeps on the stone, he has a revelatory dream. God appears to Jacob in his dream and promises him the abundant blessings of his forefathers. God makes it known to Jacob that he has a divine protector who will faithfully accompany him – a reassuring promise for Jacob who has spiritually reached a "hard place".

When Jacob wakes up from the dream, he recognises that the place he is at is a sacred place where God dwells as he proclaims, "Surely the Lord is in this place – and I did not know it!" Not only is Jacob awakened physically, but also spiritually.

How can Jacob's story speak to the story of survivors of sexual abuse? Does it have some meaning for us?

The moments of feeling vulnerable, and finding ourselves in very hard places, is not at all unusual for survivors of sexual abuse. Over and over again, we can find ourselves in spiritual spaces where we are surrounded by darkness and intense feelings of fear, pain, confusion, anxiety and despair. Although naturally, we would like to flee from these hard places, often we have no choice but to "stay". Like Jacob, we find ourselves sleeping on the "stones" that are in the hard places we arrive at – sleeping with despair… with fear… and with the hard issues we are facing.

Recently, I was speaking to a young survivor of sexual abuse who was sharing her trauma with me of revealing this for the first time to her family. The perpetrator was her father. She chose to reveal this first to her mother, and to her only sibling, her sister. She had hoped that both would believe and support her. Sadly, as she spoke about some of her traumatic memories of the event, she was strongly challenged by both who did not believe her and questioned her. She came out feeling "ripped apart!" As this young woman shared, I felt her grief. In her attempt to break years of silence and carry a heavy burden, she found herself at this very hard place to be and "sleeping on stones" of sorrow, despair and isolation.

As we sleep on these "stones" and "stay" in these "hard places", like Jacob, we may not realise that we are in a sacred space and that "God is in this place". However, God is there. God has been at all the hard places with us in the past, God is there with us now and God will be with us at all the "hard places" in the future. No matter what the hard place is for us: sorrow, despair, confusion, or fear… God is with us at this place and God "stays" with us. If we listen closely to our heart, God promises us the same thing he promised Jacob, "Know that I am with you and I will keep you wherever you go… I will not leave you…"

It is precisely in these hard places that we can experience the closeness of God to us and like Jacob, awaken to the spiritual experience that "Surely God is in this place – and I did not know it!"

When you next feel sorrow, take the opportunity to ask God, "Where are you now, God?" Listen to your heart. Does not God say to you, I am right here with you in your sorrow?

When you next feel despair, or confusion, or betrayal, you may want to ask God, "Where are you now, God? Again, listen. Doesn't God say to you, I am with you in your despair! I am with you in your confusion! I am with you as you feel betrayed! Although these experiences are terribly painful, they are opportunities to realise, "God is in this place – and I did not know it!"

How beautiful it is to be awakened to the sacred spaces that we tread within! As we enter these spaces and recognise the Presence of the Divine, things within us begin to change, shifts begin to happen, even we ourselves will be surprised. You may like to continue to "watch this space" and experience it for yourself!

Experiencing the Scripture through visualisation and art
(Suggested materials: an A4 or A3 drawing book, crayons, paints or coloured pencils)

1. You may like to title the page: Hard Places – Sacred Spaces.
2. Divide your page in half by drawing a line down it.

3. Try to picture this Scripture scene (Genesis 28) in your mind.
4. On the left hand side of your page, try to draw what the scene looks like to you
5. Looking at your drawing, what impacts you or what does it communicate to you? You may want to write this in a few words under/around your picture.
6. Now take some time to reflect on what the Genesis Scripture reading may be saying to you. Remember, Jacob was at a hard place on his journey and this "certain place" where he chose to lay his "head on a stone" was a sacred space. Are you currently at a hard place on your journey? Can you name this hard place? (It may be an issue or an intense emotion or feeling you are experiencing). If you are not in a hard place now, can you name some of the hard places you "stayed" at in the past?
7. On the right hand side of your page:
    i) Using the wider brim of a glass, trace a circle onto your page
    ii) Inside the circle, draw the "hard place(s)" you are at currently or that you have been at in the past? If you like, you can represent these hard places by drawing stones. You may like to name each of these "hard places" in a word or two under the stone
    iii) On the outside of the circle and following the circle shape, you may like to write the words that Jacob proclaimed: "The Lord is in this place – and I did not know it!"
    iv) You might like then to draw a big heart around what you have drawn so that it appears that the heart is containing everything. You may like to write your name around the heart: For example – Jane's heart.
8. Take some time to look at what you have drawn. What impacts you about your drawing? What does it communicate to you about God? Does your picture present an image of God that is different to your

previous image? For example: perhaps your drawing presents an image of God that is *with us* in suffering. Previously, you may have thought that God is far away from us when we suffer and doesn't care.

9. You may like to write a few words around your drawing that portray what you understand.

Next time you come to a hard place on your journey, you may like to come back to this Scripture, read it slowly, take time to ponder it and then look at your drawing and remember what God has communicated to you.

Awesome Miracles

Pharaoh was already near when the Israelites looked up and saw that the Egyptians were on the march in pursuit of them. In great fright they cried out to the Lord. And they complained to Moses, "Were there no burial places in Egypt that you had to bring us out here to die in the desert? Why did you do this to us? Why did you bring us out of Egypt? Did we not tell you this in Egypt, when we said, 'Leave us alone. Let us serve the Egyptians'? Far better for us to be the slaves of the Egyptians than to die in the desert." But Moses answered the people, "Fear not! Stand your ground, and you will see the victory the Lord will win for you today. These Egyptians whom you see today you will never see again. The Lord himself will fight for you; you have only to keep still."

Then the Lord said to Moses, "Why are you crying out to me? Tell the Israelites to go forward. And you, lift up your staff and, with hand outstretched over the sea, split the sea in two, that the Israelites may pass through it on dry land...

Then Moses stretched out his hand over the sea, and the Lord swept the sea with a strong east wind throughout the night and so turned it into dry land. When the water was thus divided, the Israelites marched into the midst of the sea on dry land, with the water like a wall to their right and to their left...

Thus the Lord saved Israel on that day from the power of the Egyptians.

Exodus 14:10-16; 21-22; 30a

THIS IS A VIVID AND dramatic account of an awesome miracle! We can feel the intense emotion as the people of Israel, pursued by the Egyptians, arrive to what they believe is a dead end – a "No Exit" situation – as they come to the edge of the mighty Red Sea.

Full of "great fright" that they are about to die, they cry out to the Lord and to their leader Moses, "Why did you bring us out here to die in the desert?" feeling that it would have been "far better" for them "to be slaves of the Egyptians" than "to die in the desert".[17]

Their situation was so critical that they longed again for their life of captivity and oppression, in opposition to the painful desert journey they had done so far under the leadership of Moses; one they had often complained about to him.[18] Their cries to Moses reflect their deeper search for meaning, 'What has it all been for? Has it been to arrive to this end?'

In their distress, Moses tells them, "Fear not! Stand your ground and you will see the victory the Lord will win for you today. These Egyptians whom you see today you will never see again".

Standing at the edge of death, Moses challenges their faith in God and tells them that their situation is about to change because their oppressors (the Egyptians) are going to be completely eradicated from their lives forever! No doubt a very desirable thought for the Israelites but they were probably shaking their heads and saying to themselves, "Are you for real! We are about to die!" Moses is clear with them, "The Lord himself will fight for you; you have only to keep still!"

---

17   Exodus 3:4-17. God appears to Moses through a burning bush and tells Moses "I have witnessed the affliction of my people in Egypt and have heard their cry of complaint against their slave drivers so I know well what they are suffering. Therefore I have come down to rescue them from the hands of the Egyptians and lead them out of that land into a good and spacious land, a land flowing with milk and honey". God calls Moses and commends him with this mission; "Come, now! I will send you to Pharaoh to lead my people the Israelites out of Egypt".
18   See Exodus 5:1-22 (they complain to Moses that he has made things worse for them with Pharaoh), Exodus 14:11-12 (they complain to Moses "Let us alone"), Exodus 15:22 (they complain about the bitter water), Exodus 16:1-4 (they complain about being hungry).

Then the impossible happens as God works a miracle through Moses. As Moses lifts up his staff[19] and stretches his hand over the sea, the ordinary becomes extraordinary. The sea splits in two and as God swept the sea with a strong east wind it turns into dry land enabling the Israelites to pass through it "with the water like a wall to their right and to their left".

Truly it is an awesome miracle! The great sea that had originally meant death and the end for the Israelites has been turned into a pathway to salvation through the power of God manifested through Moses' staff.

What a "terrifyingly" wonderful experience it must have been for the Israelites to see "the Lord himself fighting" for them as they see their oppressors left for dead and they walk to safety.

Is a miracle as awesome as this possible for survivors of sexual abuse or for anyone who is going through a painful experience in their life?

Through this Scripture reading, God invites us to believe so. Like the Israelites, aren't there many times on our journey of processing the sexual abuse (be it in sessions of professional counselling or psychology or when we are working through issues on our own) that we feel we have arrived at a dead end or a "no exit" situation? Aren't there times when we feel the power of our oppressors overwhelming us? The oppressors for the Israelites were the Egyptians. Who are our oppressors? They can be anyone or anything that stirs or triggers in us the memory of the sexual abuse, threatening to rob us of life: the perpetrator, flashbacks[20], panic attacks[21], nightmares... and we can complete our own list.

---

19 Moses' staff is first mentioned in the Book of Exodus 4:2-5 when God appears to Moses in the burning bush. God asks what Moses has in his hand, and Moses answers "a staff". The staff is miraculously transformed into a snake and then back into a staff. God says to Moses "This will take place so that they may believe that the Lord, the God of their fathers, the God of Abraham, the God of Isaac, the God of Jacob, did appear to you."

20 The re-emergence of a traumatic memory as a vivid recollection of sounds, images and sensations associated with the trauma. The person having the flashback typically feels as if they are re-living the event

21 A panic attack is a sudden onset of intense apprehension, fear or terror. The intense fear is inappropriate for the circumstances in which it is occurring. The symptoms experienced can be similar to those of a heart attack: racing heart, sweating, shortness of breath, chest pain, dizziness, body weakness, feeling detached from oneself, and a sense of losing control. Panic attacks are a common issue in survivors of sexual abuse.

Often, when we feel overwhelmed, we ask the same questions that the Israelites did: What is this all for? Will I ever make it out of this journey safely? These questions lead us to search for deeper meaning.

In the same way that God heard the questioning cries of the Israelites, God hears us. In our search for meaning, God speaks to us through this Scripture and invites us to believe in our distress, "the Lord himself will fight for you, you have only to keep still."

The "stillness" that God is inviting us to is "stillness" within ourselves. We "do" so much work in processing past events but this Scripture invites us to simply "be" – be present. As we focus on "being", not only do we become more aware of the thoughts and emotions that are racing through our mind and heart, we also become aware of the Sacred; that is that God is "in this place" (as talked about in the previous chapter), a "place" of "no exit" or a "dead end" situation. It is "in this place" that God promises you "The Lord himself will fight for you".

The Israelites experienced the all-powerful God fighting for them through the "staff" of Moses. As Moses held up the "staff", the dead end and "no exit" situation they had arrived to turned into a pathway to salvation.

We do not have a "staff" but we have the gift of faith in God. Our faith in God is a very powerful tool that can turn any dead end or no exit situation into an experience of salvation. It empowers us to walk safely through terrifying situations. These are the miracles that God can perform in our life through faith.

So as we continue to walk our healing journey, we are invited to raise our "staff", that is, to let our faith in God rise in our hearts and to believe that God is fighting for us against our oppressors, allowing us to come forward safely and exit what we previously experienced as a dead end situation.

What a powerful tool we hold in our hands; a tool that will enable us to experience miracles in our life again and again. Whenever you feel you're at a dead end or that there is no way out of a situation, raise up your "staff"; that is your faith in God and let God do the miracle in your life for you.

Experiencing the Scripture through visualisation and art
(Suggested materials: an A4 or A3 drawing book, crayons, paints or coloured pencils)

1. You may like to title the page: Awesome Miracles.
2. Spend some time reflecting on who or what oppresses you. You may want to write it down in a journal.
3. The Israelites originally saw the "sea" as a dead end and no exit situation. Imagine what the Israelites would have felt as they arrived at this place.
    i) What emotions do you experience when you arrive at situations and feel that there is no way out (fear, hopelessness, powerlessness, frustration....)? You may like to write these down.

   For this activity, it may be helpful to view these emotions as the impossible "sea" in your life that you feel you cannot cross through safely.
4. As you recall these emotions, give yourself time to acknowledge God's loving presence "in this place".
    i) You may want to ask God, "Where are you now?" Allow God to remind you "I am in this place" (Genesis 28:16)... I am in your fear... I am in your hopelessness.
5. Spend time listening to God who assures you through this Scripture reading, "*I myself will fight for you; you have only to keep still.*" Absorb God's Word and allow yourself to experience God's loving care and protection.
6. Take time now to acknowledge the powerful tool you hold in your hands – your faith in God. This is your "staff". By "raising your staff" you will experience God's power and grace to work awesome miracles in your life.

   Try to imagine the scene where Moses raises his staff and outstretches his hand over the water and it divides.

Now try to imagine your "sea" as you recalled it in question 3i). Allow God to invite you through Scripture to "raise your staff" over the "sea" of emotions in your heart, that is, hold your faith in God's loving care and powerful protection above your fear… hold it above your hopelessness.

7. Try to imagine as you do, your impossible sea dividing… that is a pathway being created through your fear and your hopelessness. Notice how you feel as you imagine this.
8. Allow God to invite you through the words of Scripture to "Come forward!" and to walk safely through this sea, that is, "Come forward through your fear… through your despair…"
9. Imagine yourself crossing through the impossible sea of emotions in your heart and reaching the other side safely. As you look behind you and realise what you have crossed through, how do you feel (grateful, awe-struck, faith-filled, empowered, strengthened, light-hearted)?
10. You may like to spend time capturing in a drawing what you imagine as you stand on the other side and look at the impossible sea of emotions that you have crossed.
11. Take some time now to look at your drawing.
    i) You may want to name things on it, for example, name your oppressors, name the emotions that represent your sea, name the feelings as you stand on the other side.
12. As you look at your drawing, what does it communicate to you about God (for example, God cares for me, God can do impossible things in my life, God is powerful…)?

You may like to put a few words around your drawing that reflect this.

Perhaps this changes your image of God in some way. If this is so, take time to acknowledge this. What image of God does this new image invite you to let go of?

Remember that your faith in THIS God is your "staff"; it is a powerful tool that can do impossible miracles in your life. Next time you arrive to an impossible situation where you feel there is no way out... come back to this drawing and let God remind you to "raise up your staff over the sea" and see the powerful miracles that God can do in you.

Carried not Dumped[22]

In the wilderness, you saw how the Lord God carried you, just as one carries a child, all the way that you have travelled until you have reached this place.

Deuteronomy 1:31

RECENTLY, MY MOTHER WAS SHARING with me some of her fond, early childhood memories. She remembered accompanying her parent's visits to other family members where they would enjoy playing a game of cards together. She expressed how the walks going and coming from their place were too long for her because she was only a small child. She remembers complaining and crying to her father along the way saying, "Dad, it's too far and I am too tired to walk!" Without hesitation her father would tenderly pick her up and carry her home on his shoulders. My mother's eyes lit up as she shared these memories and I noticed that she did not focus on the challenges of the journey but rather emphasised with delight the tender care of her father who wanted to make the journey easy and pleasant for her.

While the integrity of this beautiful imagery depicts the characteristics of tender loving care and support, this may not be so for survivors of childhood abuse whose strongest memories of being "carried" as a child may be associated with traumatic events. As survivors try to sit with the image of God "carrying us as one carries a child", perhaps feelings of rebelliousness, distrust, repulsiveness, fear, anxiety and even anger may arise; that is, the very same feelings and emotions that were experienced at the time of the sexual abuse. Along with

---

22 For some survivors, the imagery of being carried may trigger some painful memories that I will address in this chapter. I invite survivors to discern if you feel it is appropriate or not for you to engage with this chapter. You may like to work through this chapter with a support person or in a professional therapy session.

these feelings we may have the reaction, "I don't want to be carried by God. I don't want God to touch me or to come anywhere near me! I can't trust God!" We may find it difficult to understand why we are feeling and reacting to God like this but what we are doing here is reacting and responding to God with the same feelings and attitudes that we had towards our perpetrator.

These feelings may be even more pronounced if our perpetrator was a member of the clergy and someone whom we referred to as "Father". In psychological terms, this reaction is described as 'transference'[23]. Unconsciously, we associate the feelings and reactions that belong to our perpetrator (Father X for some) with God. It is at this very point that we experience the grave spiritual harm of sexual abuse, particularly abuse by a member of the clergy. Sexual abuse by clergy gravely taints our image of God, particularly God as Father. The distortion of our image of God as Father is so great that for some survivors, the image of a loving God is unreachable and unbelievable. If we are talking about God as our Father, and our perpetrator was either our own father or a Reverend whom we referred to as 'father', then sadly, the image we adopt of God as Father, will be the image of Father X or our own father. This is an indication of how sexual abuse gravely harms and destroys the spiritual and faith dimension of survivors. Rather than this Scripture providing survivors with the security and assurance of God's constant and eternal love and care, it may create panic and chaos.

If this does occur for you, you may find it helpful to work through the steps of the footnote that I will later provide for you. These steps will help you to be attentive to what is happening within you as you try to read and spend time with this Scripture reading. Through the grace of God and with gentle persistence, I have experienced that it is possible to correct the distorted image that we have of God as "Father" as a consequence of sexual abuse.

In this sense, we will be able to identify very well with the Israelites who struggled to believe that God loved them and wanted the very best for them. Their image of God was also a very tainted one; they believed God "hated"

---

23 Sigmund Freud described transference as that part of therapy when the patient unconsciously substitutes the physician for a person from the patient's past. In our present context, this can mean transferring feelings and emotions associated with the perpetrator of our traumatic past on to God.

them and wanted to "destroy" them.[24] Moses had a very different image and experience of God. He knew God to be tender, loving and caring; a God who carries us and doesn't dump us. Moses invites the Israelites to know God as God is - Love.

This scene from Scripture takes place after the Israelites have been on a very long and challenging journey through the "great" and "terrible wilderness" in pursuit of the land "promised" to them by God[25]. When they finally reach the Promised Land, they refuse to enter. The experience of God's goodness is so close at hand yet their mistrust of God is preventing them from tasting it. They complain to Moses, "The people are stronger and taller than we and the cities are large and fortified up to Heaven!" (Deuteronomy 1:24-28a).

It is in this context that Moses begs the Israelites, "Have no dread or fear of them. The Lord your God, who goes before you, is the one who will fight for you, just as he did for you in Egypt before your very eyes and in the wilderness where you saw how the Lord your God carried you, just as one carries a child, all the way that you travelled until you reached this place" (Deuteronomy 1:29-31).

Even though the Israelites had experienced the saving power of God abundantly, right from the Exodus from Egypt and in the wilderness, it happened to them what can happen to us – their minds and hearts were clouded by their distorted image of God and this prevented them from knowing God as God is: tender, loving, and caring enough to carry us and not abandon and dump us on the way! We are invited through this Scripture to know God as God is!

While we may all be at a different "place" on our healing journey, there is no doubt that for each of us, processing the traumatic events of our past can be compared to wandering in a vast "wilderness"; there is no clear pathway mapped out for us to walk. Often, we find ourselves lost, with no sense of direction and purpose, stumbling upon challenge after challenge, not seeing anything with clarity ahead of us. We find ourselves often thinking, 'will we ever come out

---

24   Deuteronomy 1:27
25   Exodus 3:8 "Therefore, I have come down to rescue them from the hands of the Egyptians and lead them out of that land, into a good and spacious land, a land flowing with milk and honey, the country of the Canaanites, Hittites, Amorites, Perizzites, Hivites and Jebusites."

of this' to experience a "good and spacious land" – the same land that God promised to the Israelites?

We may not be aware but we are not alone in the "wilderness" of our healing journey. Whether we realise it or not, God is carrying us, not with the same intentions of our perpetrators but "just as one carries a child"; that is, the way a truly authentic father would carry his own child – with tender loving care – and not only for a short part of the journey but "all the way that you have travelled until you have reached this place".

It's such a beautiful image! Imagine the feelings that are connected with being "carried" by someone you totally trust when you are totally exhausted and can't do anymore? Can you imagine the relief, the gratitude, the happiness, and the renewed hope that you would experience? Imagine how loved and esteemed you would feel that someone cares enough to carry you!

It can happen that we look back over our healing journey in retrospect and we think to ourselves, "How did I ever get through that?" or "How did I get to this point?" or "Where did I get my strength from?" Perhaps others feel they are not able to look back over their journey like this yet but whether we recognise it or not, God has carried us, "just as one carries a child, all the way that you have travelled until you have reached this place". God has loved you generously, constantly, lovingly, tenderly and with so much care and sensitivity.

Not only has God been with you in every challenge and obstacle but God has felt your fatigue, despair, hopelessness and powerlessness. God never ever dumps us on our journey; on the contrary, God picks us up and carries us. If you find yourself asking, "How did I ever come through that?" or "How did I get to this point?" It's by God's grace – God has carried you "all the way that you have travelled until you have reached this place" where you stand at this point in time.

You may like to spend some more time creatively absorbing the reality of a "loving' God through art.

Experiencing the Scripture through visualisation and art
(Suggested materials: an A4 or A3 drawing book, crayons, paints or coloured pencils)

1. You may like to title the page: Carried not dumped.
2. Read slowly the words of Deuteronomy 1:31, being aware that God speaks to us when we read God's Word in the Bible[26], that is, we listen to God when we read God's Word in the Bible.

   If the imagery of the Scripture triggers traumatic memories for you, you may like to work through the steps below[27] in the footnote. You may like to repeat these steps whenever you experience you are doing a "transference" on God as you read the Scriptures. If practised with patience, these steps facilitate us to disentangle the unhelpful image of God that we have adopted as a consequence of the spiritual harm that has been caused by our perpetrator.
3. You may like to depict your healing journey by drawing what you visualise your "wilderness" looks like (you may want to use a couple of pages for this activity). Take advantage of colours to capture your feelings and emotions.

   i) Spend time reflecting on what the challenges, obstacles and achievements have been for you right

---

[26] Documents of the Second Vatican Council, *Dei Verbum, Dogmatic Constitution on Divine Revelation*, #25.

[27] In the case that you would like to continue but experience painful memories or flashbacks, you may find that working through the following steps is helpful to overcome some of the spiritual impacts that sexual abuse has had on your relationship with God: 1. Was there a particular thought that came to your mind or did you experience a flashback? 2. As this came to you, what were you feeling? (Anxiety, fear, terror…) 3. Try to identify who these thoughts, flashbacks, or feelings refer to? (For example, your perpetrator) 4. Once you have identified who your responses refer to, try to be aware that now you are in the presence of God who is Love and not in the presence of your perpetrator. Some self-talk may be helpful, for example, "I am safe! I am not with my perpetrator. I am with God who is Love. God is not like my perpetrator and not my perpetrator. God and my perpetrator are very different." 5. You may want to tell God how you feel as you try to imagine God "carrying" you. (For example, God I am so afraid to imagine myself being "carried" by you!). 6. Try to silence all the noises in your heart and let God assure you "I am God and not your perpetrator!" 7. If you feel calm enough, you may want to proceed with the activity.

up until today (the idea is that you will end up drawing a path of issues through the wilderness).

ii) Include them by illustrating/marking them in your "wilderness" so that you understand its significance for you.

iii) As you look at each challenge/obstacle/achievement that you have drawn, if there was one emotion or feeling that you had to say you were experiencing at the time, what would it be (e.g. sadness, despair…)? Write that word next to the particular issue.

4. As you spend time pondering the picture you have drawn, re-read the words of Scripture:

In the wilderness, you saw how the Lord God carried you, just as one carries a child, all the way that you have travelled until you have reached this place.

Looking one by one at your obstacles and challenges, you may like to ask God, "Were you truly carrying me at that place?"

5. In your drawing, if you had to represent God carrying you all the way through the wilderness up until today, how would you draw it? You may like to do this.

6. As you look at your drawing, what does it communicate to you about God?

You may like to put a few words around your drawing that reflect this.

How does what you have drawn change your image of God? What image of God does this new image invite you to let go of?

Next time you are finding it difficult to trust God, or you feel that God doesn't care, you may like to come back to this picture to remind yourself of who God really is: someone who cares enough to "carry you" with tender love, particularly when you strike obstacles and challenges.

Divinely Loved[28]

Yes, the Lord has chosen Zion, desired it for a dwelling: "This is my resting place forever, here I will dwell, for I desire it."

Psalm 132:13-14

THESE VERSES FROM SCRIPTURE ARE part of a royal psalm celebrating God's election of Zion and the sanctuary there as the divine abode on earth.[29] "Zion" is in Jerusalem and it is on Mount Zion that David built a citadel. Zion here is also synonymous with people of Zion. This verse of Scripture reveals God's love for the people of Zion and the choice for it to be "God's dwelling" - "a resting place" for God "forever".

There is a saying, "home is where the heart is". God's heart is with the people of Zion and so much so, that God chooses to make a home with them.

---

28   The language or use of particular words in this Scripture may trigger traumatic memories for survivors which will be dealt with in this chapter. I will leave it to the discretion of survivors to decide whether or not they feel ready to proceed.

29   The Sanctuary will lodge the Ark of the Covenant, also called 'ark of the Lord', 'ark of God', 'ark of the covenant of the Lord' (Deuteronomy 10:8) and 'ark of the testimony'. The ark was a rectangular box made of acacia wood, and measured 2 1/2 x 1 1/2 x 1 1/2 cubits (i.e. c. 4 x 2 1/2 x 2 1/2 feet or c. 1.22 m x 76 cm x 76 cm). The whole was covered with gold and was carried on poles inserted in rings at the four lower corners. The lid, or 'mercy-seat', was a gold plate surrounded by two antithetically placed cherubs with outspread wings.

The ark served (i) as receptacle for the two tablets of the Decalogue (Exodus 25:16, 21; 40:20; Deuteronomy 10:1-5) and also for the pot of manna and Aaron's rod (Hebrews 9:4-5); (ii) as the meeting-place in the inner sanctuary where the Lord revealed his will to his servants (Moses: Exodus 25:22; 30:36; Aaron: Leviticus 16:2; Joshua: Joshua 7:6). Thus it served as the symbol of the divine presence guiding his people.

After finding the Ark of the Covenant in the old sanctuary in Kiriath-jearim (1 Samuel 7:1-2), King David swears an oath to build a new sanctuary for the Lord, "I will not give sleep to my eyes or slumber to my eyelids, until I find a place for the Lord, a dwelling place for the Mighty One of Jacob" (Psalm 132:5). David has set up this new shrine to lodge the Ark of Covenant in Jerusalem.

Take a moment to ponder what that means! God – the God of all Life and Love - is looking for a home; a place where God can rest forever, a permanent dwelling place. We are not talking here about any ordinary human being looking for a place to live but we are talking about our extraordinary God; the all-powerful God – the Divine Being. God could choose to live anywhere God wants to be but out of all the places on earth God choses Zion.

Imagine the privilege and honour the people of Zion would have felt to know themselves to be the dwelling place and home of God! For the fact of their past history, being a people severely broken through the Babylonian destruction of Jerusalem and their temple (587 BCE), this honour would have been felt even more. Yet, their past history and their brokenness is not even a slight issue for God in choosing to dwell with them. Zion is the place where God wants to be forever - so great is God's love for Zion that they are divinely loved.

Imagine how elated Zion would have felt knowing that they were chosen to be God's dwelling place. What importance… what esteem… what worthiness… what love they would have experienced! How ecstatic they would have been to experience that despite their past sufferings, losses, griefs, humiliations, God still held them not only worthy of divine love but worthy to be God's divine dwelling place. One could imagine that all their past hang-ups, complaints, complexes, grievances, would fall away in such a way that as a people they were no longer defined by the tragic past events of their life but by the truth of who they were for God – *God's resting place forever*. How divinely loved was Zion!

So how can this Scripture (Psalm 132) relate to survivors of sexual abuse? I am certain that reading this particular Scripture will prove to be challenging for survivors due to the language, particularly the words: "chosen", "desired it", and "a resting place".

Often, survivors of sexual abuse were told by their perpetrators that they are the "special one", the "favourite", the "loveliest", the "chosen one". Sadly, these words were part of the perpetrators grooming tactics in an attempt to win our trust as children and to make us feel that we were safe while with them. Even years after the traumatic events have ceased, their memories can be stirred up by language, that is: words, expressions, tones, and even the language of silence. Even as adults, if survivors are told by someone, "You are special", or "You are my favourite", or "I have chosen you", strong feelings of terror, repulsion, anxiety, anger, and rebelliousness can be stirred up. Even if these words are used appropriately and with integrity, the reaction of a survivor may confuse the person who spoke the words and and they may think, "What did I say wrong? What did I do that caused such a reaction?" The issue at hand for the survivor is the language that has been used; a language that is associated with our traumatic past. Healing these effects can take time and patience.

If reading this Scripture unsettles you with flashbacks or traumatic memories, you may like to follow the steps below in the footnote and as mentioned in previous chapters.[30] Repeatedly working through these steps will enable us to not transfer the feelings towards our perpetrator on to God and it will empower us to engage in a life-giving and loving relationship with God.

The important thing for us to know is that when God speaks to us through Scripture, God's Word always comes to us from a place of authentic Love, for "God is Love" (1 John 4:8). Although our first reaction when we read the words from this Scripture may be: "I don't want to be God's chosen one" and "I don't want God to desire me"… "I want God to stay as far away as possible from me because being the "chosen one" will mean being abused", hopefully, by understanding that we are doing a transference, we will eventually be able to receive God's Word from a place of Love.

If we are able to do this, God's message to us from this Scripture is one that can make a huge difference in our life. When you read it slowly, replace the words "Zion" and "it" with your own name. As you let the words sink in you will

---

[30] In the case that you would like to continue but experience painful memories or flashbacks, you may find that working through the following steps is helpful to overcome some of the spiritual impacts that sexual abuse has had on your relationship with God: 1. Was there a particular thought that came to your mind or did you experience a flashback? 2. As this came to you, what were you feeling? (Anxiety, fear, terror…) 3. Try to identify who these thoughts, flashbacks, or feelings refer to? (For example, your perpetrator) 4. Once you have identified who your responses refer to, try to be aware that now you are in the presence of God who is Love and not in the presence of your perpetrator. Some self-talk may be helpful, for example, "I am safe! I am not with my perpetrator. I am with God who is Love. God is not like my perpetrator and not my perpetrator. God and my perpetrator are very different." 5. You may want to tell God how you feel as you listen to God telling you that you are the "chosen" one. (For example, God I am so scared when you tell me I am your "chosen" one!). 6. Try to silence all the noises in your heart and let God assure you "I am God and not your perpetrator!" 7. If you feel calm enough, you may want to proceed with the activity.

experience that God is communicating a message of great love to you. In the same way that God's heart longed to be with the people of Zion, God's heart longs to be with you! God loves you so much that God wants to be one with you – God wants you to be "God's resting place forever!" In the New Testament, Paul, in his first letter to the Corinthians, makes us aware that this is already reality: "Don't you know that you yourselves are God's temple and that God's Spirit dwells in your midst?"[31] God is intimately involved with us – we are God's temple and "resting place forever" and we never need to be afraid because "God is Love"[32] that is, Love is God's nature. This is the reason why we never need to be afraid of God because God will never hurt us, hate us or try to destroy us because this would go against God's nature of Love. God could never ever desire that any evil come upon us because it goes against God's nature.

But survivors of clerical abuse will ask, "How is it that someone who was supposed to represent God and love like God did such an evil thing to me that has destroyed my life?" "If a priest abused me, won't God?" Over and over again we find ourselves grappling with these lingering questions. Sadly, they reflect the grave spiritual harm that has been caused to the faith of survivors of clerical abuse.

What needs to be reiterated is that sexual abuse is an evil act that goes against the true nature of God who is Love. This is the reason why the act of sexual abuse is never an act of God. Sexual abuse by a member of the clergy or religious life is the act of a human being who is called to be a reflection of God's Love but instead chooses to act upon the evil that has seduced the human heart. The evil act of sexual abuse is the consequence of evil working in/through a human heart but it is not an act of God who is Love. In the case of perpetrators who were/are "religious", it is the act of one who has gone very far away from the core of their religious calling; that is, to be and to live the Love of God for others.

We may ask, "Does God care that this happened to me?" Over the years, I have repeatedly brought this question to God. God is profoundly grieved by these acts of evil. No one ever wants to see those they love and care for

---

31   1 Corinthians 3:16
32   1 John 4:8

hurt! When we do, we feel their pain and heart-ache. How much more does God, who created us from dust, and who breathed the breath of Life into us, and who loves us more profoundly than any other human being can possibly ever love us, feel grieved to see us so gravely harmed by these crimes. God is even more grieved to see that the people who committed these evil acts were precisely the people that God called to be a reflection of the Divine Love for others. They are the people God called to care for the flock and protect them from danger… supposedly they were to be role models of the "Good Shepherd" who came to give life in abundance but instead they turned out to be "thieves and robbers" and "the hired hand who does not care for the sheep" [33]. God is profoundly grieved by all the harm caused through this evil act, not only to survivors, but to their family members, their friends and those supporting them, to congregations, and to all those who hear of these evil acts and suffer the loss of their faith, hope and love in God.

It speaks for itself why we can easily identify with the people of Zion in this Scripture. Like them, we too have been severely broken by our past history due to the grave harm done to us by our perpetrators. However, through the words of this Scripture reading, God invites us not to be defined by the tragedies of our past: the sufferings, losses, humiliations, and grief that is a consequence of it but to be defined by who we are for God – we are God's "resting place forever" – God's dwelling place – God's temple.

Our story of tragedy does not prevent God from divinely loving us. We have been, we are, and we will always be divinely loved by God who is constantly pouring out divine Love in our life. God's has divinely loved you before you were abused, during the sexual abuse, and after the traumatic events stopped, all the way along your healing journey until you have reached the place you are at now.

Survivors find it so challenging to allow ourselves to be loved by others, let alone God. One of the effects of sexual abuse is that it shapes the way we feel and think about ourselves. For example, a survivor can struggle for years feeling that they "are" a "bad" person who did "bad" things, until we learn to differentiate that just because "bad things" were done to me doesn't make me a bad person.

---

[33] John 10:10; 12

The "bad" was the evil that manifested in the heart of the perpetrator and we have been a victim of that badness. Or we may feel we are unlovable because of the multiple damaging effects of the sexual abuse in our life and experiencing these effects, makes us hate ourselves. It's normal to hate the effects that can make us "feel" unlovable at times but just because we "feel" unlovable doesn't mean that we "are" unlovable.

Even though we cannot love ourselves, God can and does! God loves us even more than we love ourselves. We struggle to understand this, asking, "How can God love me when I hate myself? How can you love me when I feel so unlovable?"

God gave each one of us life because God loved us. Our existence is not some "bad mistake" or "an accident". Our life has been willed by God's Love, long before abuse was ever a part of our history! You are divinely loved by God who has made you God's "resting place".

Yes, God rests in you and divinely loves you in every moment of your day even when you are unaware of it: be it if you are sitting down, rising up to walk, thinking, lying down, in your travels.[34] God divinely loves you when you feel fatigued, hopeless, disappointed, wasted, angry, despairing. There is not a moment in your life when God does not divinely love you. This is such an awesome truth yet we spend so little time pondering on it.

If we can challenge ourselves to spend some time pondering on this every day in our life, then, gradually, we may experience that the tragic events of our past will no longer define us but what will is who we are for God – God's resting place – the place where God lives and the place where God loves us divinely. There will never be a greater reality to experience in our life-time than this one.

May this truth of our faith transform and define our life more, and more, as we come to believe and experience it.

---

34   Psalm 139:2-3

Experiencing the Scripture through visualisation and art
(Suggested materials: an A4 or A3 drawing book, crayons, paints or coloured pencils)

1. You may like to title the page: Divinely Loved.
2. Read slowly the words of Psalm 132:13-14, being aware that God speaks to us when we read God's Word in the Bible.[35]
   (If this triggers traumatic memories for you, you may like to follow the steps of Footnote 30.)
3. What does being divinely loved look like for you? Try to draw this if you can. You may like to write a few key words around your picture that capture its meaning for you.
4. As you look at your drawing, what does it communicate to you about God?
   How does your drawing change your image of God? You may like to write this in a few words on your drawing.
   Is there an "old" image of God that this "new" image is inviting you to let go of?

Whenever you feel unlovable or feelings of self-hate begin to arise, you may like to come back to this Scripture and drawing and allow God to communicate through it that you are divinely loved forever.

---

[35] Documents of the Second Vatican Council, *Dei Verbum, Dogmatic Constitution on Divine Revelation*, #25.

Blessed Mountain

*On this mountain the L*ORD *of hosts will make for all*
    peoples
a feast of rich food, a feast of well-aged wines
of rich food filled with marrow, of well-aged wines
    strained clear
And he will destroy on this mountain
the shroud that is cast over all peoples,
the sheet that is spread over all nations;
he will swallow up death forever.
*Then the Lord G*OD *will wipe away the tears from all*
    faces,
and the disgrace of his people he will take away from all
    the earth,
*for the L*ORD *has spoken.*

Isaiah 25:6-8

FOR SURVIVORS OF SEXUAL ABUSE, the process of healing can feel like climbing a very steep mountain. As we climb, our whole being is consumed: physically, emotionally, mentally, psychologically and spiritually. There are constant challenges facing us along the way and issues that require both inner and outer work (Part II will deal with some of these). We get weary, our body grows weak, and often we feel lifeless. Mentally and psychologically it's a tough journey and the temptations plague us and make us feel: "I'll never get to the end of it!", "I can't do it anymore!", "What's it all for!"

Temptations try to convince us to give up. They drive us into very dark places and trick us into feeling that we have no hope of healing. They play with our minds, telling us there's nothing "good" to look forward to in the future. Temptations are lies that try very hard to seduce us into believing them. Perhaps one of the reasons why temptations get the better of us is because we cannot see an end in sight to conquer the mountain; if only we could say, "by the end of this year I will reach the top and this climb will be over!" it would be such a huge psychological relief. But this isn't so! The climbing process is an arduous and slow one that happens in our everyday lives as we face the individual challenges that arise along the way; each challenge is a wilderness in itself; a venture into the unknown where no visible pathway exists. Creating a pathway takes time; there are psychological blocks that we need to clear, connections that we need to make between triggers in our external world and our own reactions to them, and recognizing our own cognitive patterns that can prevent us from going into the wilderness.

For each survivor, the time this takes will vary but in no way does the time it takes a survivor to work through an issue ever reflect the quality of a healing journey.

This beautiful Scripture from the Prophet Isaiah offers survivors of sexual abuse abounding hope and invites us to believe that God will transform our mountain to a blessed mountain of abundance and richness and that on our mountain we will come to know God as our Saviour.

The "mountain" being referred to in these verses is "Mount Zion" – the place where God desired to dwell forever among God's people.[36] In these verses, the Prophet is recalling the ritual meal taken on Mount Sinai that served to affirm the Covenant between God and the people freed from slavery under the Egyptians.[37] It marked the people's transition from slavery in Egypt to Life with God.

In Isaiah's vision, "on this mountain", Mount Zion, the God of heaven and the whole earth will defeat the ultimate enemy, "destroying the shroud that is cast over all peoples, the sheet that is spread over all nations… swallowing up death forever." "This mountain" will be a blessed mountain where God's people will experience the faithfulness of a God who loves them deeply.

---

36 Psalm 132:13-14
37 Exodus 24:9-11

Blessed Mountain

Through the Prophet's words we can truly feel God's empathic and tender heart that knows what the people are suffering. God feels their poverty and weakness and sees their tears. God is not indifferent to their suffering but is deeply moved; so moved that God promises to wipe away the people's tears of grief and disgrace. It's such a beautiful image that portrays the maternal and paternal heart of God.

The same is true for us as we climb our mountain of healing from the effects and impacts of sexual abuse. Remember, "God is in this place"[38]. Even though we may not feel God's presence, we are not alone. Just as God was on Mount Zion, God is on our mountain; it is "God's resting place forever"[39]. God is not unaffected on our mountain. God's tender heart empathises with us in our sufferings. God feels our poverty and weakness and does not miss a single tear of grief that we shed. God is deeply moved by our suffering and promises to "wipe away all our tears" and the "disgrace" that we experience.

How is it possible when our tears run so deep and we experience multiple consequential disgraces from the trauma? Humanly speaking, it would seem impossible but as Scripture reminds us "for God, nothing is impossible"[40].

But there is even more God promises to do for us! God promises to "destroy" the "shroud" and "sheet" that is spread over us... the "sheet" that has kept this secret covered up in darkness and silence, the "sheet" that has left us feeling a heavy burden and led us to a slow spiritual death, the "sheet" that has not allowed God's light and love to enter into the place within where we are in deep need of healing. God wants to "destroy" this "shroud" and "sheet" and restore us to freedom and lightness of heart.

So, as much as we have suffered climbing our mountain, God promises us that it is a "blessed" mountain. "Blessed" because on "this mountain" God has prepared a banquet for us of "rich food" and "well-aged wines", in other words, this mountain is the place where God promises to nourish us with everything we need for our journey:life, love, light, hope, courage, joy, peace, faith, perseverance... making us rich and strong. It is a "blessed" mountain that offers

---

[38] Genesis 28:16
[39] Psalm 132:14
[40] Luke 1:37

us the experience of God's grace and closeness which will slowly transform us, turning our tears into rejoicing and our disgraces into graces to be shared with others.

It is a "blessed" mountain that tells of our unique and sacred story. God participates in our story and God will transform it and give it new life and from this life others will find courage, hope and inspiration. So the next time you are invited to "climb" this mountain, remember how blessed it is.

You may like to spend some time drawing how you envisage your "blessed" mountain, that is, your sacred story.

Experiencing the Scripture through visualisation and art
(Suggested materials: an A4 or A3 drawing book, crayons, paints or coloured pencils)

1. You may like to title the page: Blessed Mountain.
2. Read the words of this Scripture (Isaiah 25) slowly, being aware that God speaks to us when we read God's Word in the Bible.
3. On your page, you may like to draw a huge mountain. On the steep upward slope of the mountain, you may like to put your name, for example, Jane's Mountain.
4. On the base of the mountain, you may like to draw some tear drops… You may want to name each tear drop as the issues that you have shed tears for (even the silent tears). You can put as many tears as you want.
5. Just above those tears drops, you may like to draw a "sheet" or a "shroud" that is being destroyed or lifted. You may like to write a word next to it that is significant for you, for example, cover-up.
6. At the peak of the mountain, you may like to represent the banquet of richness that God is offering you on "this" mountain, that is, everything that God wants to nourish you with for your climb… Whatever you understand that to be: for example, courage, hope,

peace, patience, friendship.... You may like to write these things or draw what they look like for you.

7. Spend some time absorbing what you have drawn. How do you feel as you look at your sacred story now? In one word, how would you describe your sacred story? You may like to write this somewhere on your page.
8. What is your most prominent feeling as you look at your drawing? You may like to write this somewhere on your page.
9. As you look at your picture, how are you being invited to read your sacred story? How is this different to before? You may like to capture this in some way on your drawing.

Next time you are faced with the challenges or temptations of your "mountain", you may like to come back to this Scripture and your drawing and be reminded of how "blessed" your mountain is.

Something New

Do not remember the events of the past,
the things of long ago consider not;
See, I am doing something new!
Now it springs forth, do you not perceive it?

Isaiah 43:18-19a

WE WOULD ALL BE FAMILIAR with the saying, "the same old thing". Often, when we hear it being used, or when we use it ourselves, we hear tones of frustration, boredom, monotony and dissatisfaction. Beneath the expression, there is a longing to see change and newness in our life or the life of others.

However, when the people of Israel referred to in this Scripture, remembered "the same old thing", that is, "the events of the past" and "the things of long ago", they were not remembering bad things! "The same old thing" in their case referred to the past wondrous deeds of God during the great Exodus from Egypt. These "events of the past" were often remembered and handed down to the following generations through the means of the oral tradition. Even though these stories communicated "old" experiences of God's wonder, the people of Israel clung to them because they highlighted God's love, care, providence, protection and faithfulness towards them.

The people of Israel, in the context of this Scripture, are in exile in Babylon so we can imagine that remembering the events of the past gave them a sense of hope that just as God had been powerful all those years ago, God could be powerful again in their current situation of homelessness.

The words of this Scripture spoken through the prophet would have been such beautiful music to the ears of this people in exile. God is communicating to them through the prophet, 'Don't cling to the old experiences of my love for you… where you experienced me leading you out of captivity in Egypt… but instead see, I am doing something new!"

God is about to give the people of Israel a "new" and "fresh" experience of God's wonder and awe by breaking them out of their Babylonian exile, in a new exodus that is going to be even more glorious than the former exodus from Egypt. How enlivened the people would have felt at hearing these words and what meaning it would have added to their current situation!

This Scripture reading can speak volumes to survivors of sexual abuse.

In a way, the event of sexual abuse exiles us from the place within ourselves that we call "home" and can "be". It's the experience of not feeling well within one's own skin as we struggle to connect to self, to God and to others. Even though a long time may have passed since the traumatic events stopped, we may still feel like "foreigners" and "strangers" to ourselves, not understanding or having insight into our reactions, behaviours, thoughts, and feelings. Just like the people of Israel in this Scripture, we too are exiled and homeless.

Without a doubt, we too "remember the events of the past". However, unlike the people of Israel, what we remember again and again is the traumatic events, and this is not because we want to remember, or try to recall them, but it's because *our body remembers it* for us, constantly reminding us of it even though all we want is to forget it forever.[41]

As *our body* remembers, perhaps the memories are accompanied by "the same old things": the same old behaviours, the same old patterns, the same old thoughts, the same old feelings, and the same old reactions. We long to break the cycle of the "old" in our life with "something new".

The word God speaks to us through this Scripture is one that gives us great hope for our healing journey. God is about to break the cycle of the "old" in our life with "something new" and God invites us to look at our life closely and to "see" because this "new" thing we yearn for is already happening through the grace of God.

---

41 The traumatic memories come intrusively through nightmares and flashbacks which can manifest through a multitude of triggers such as a certain body language, a geographical place, certain smells, certain objects, items of clothing, etc.

So much of our energy can go into processing the "past events" that we don't give ourselves time to "see" and rejoice in the "new thing(s)" that is happening right now! Through this Scripture God invites you to "see" what's "new" in your life. God asks you through this Scripture, "Do you perceive it?"

Can you name the "new thing" that is flourishing in you? How or when do you "see" it "springing forth"?

Even though, in your eyes, it may only be a small "new" thing, acknowledge it as a sign of "new" life emerging in you. Perhaps it is that you are doing something "new" that you have never done before: For example – expressing your need, doing something nice for yourself, going to a place that you couldn't go to previously, behaving in a different manner, speaking out for the first time. Perhaps it is a "new" thing that is more subtle, like a shift in the way you think or feel about yourself or a situation.

After you "see" and acknowledge this "new" thing, try to celebrate it in some way no matter how small you feel it may be.

As you continue your healing journey, try to be attentive to the "new things" that happen along the way and take time to celebrate them, for they are what enliven us, encourage us, and fill us with new hope and meaning on our healing journey. More significantly, they are the manifestation of God's Presence with you.

You may like to spend some time capturing this "new" thing in your life through the activity below.

Experiencing the Scripture through visualisation and art
(Suggested materials: an A4 or A3 drawing book, crayons, paints or coloured pencils)

1. You may like to title the page: Something New.
2. Read the words of this Scripture (Isaiah 43) slowly, being aware that God speaks to us when we read God's Word in the Bible.[42]

---

42 Documents of the Second Vatican Council, *Dei Verbum, Dogmatic Constitution on Divine Revelation*, #25.

3. Reflect on the "new thing" that is emerging in you. Perhaps it is still unfolding in your life. Can you name it?
4. You may like to reflect on other "new" things that have emerged in you over the last couple of years. Try to name them.
5. On your page, try to draw a tree including the roots of the tree in the ground, its branches and its leaves. This tree represents your life. The roots of the tree represent God. No matter what sort of life our tree has had, it is still grounded in God's love. You may like to write the word God beneath the roots of your tree.

    In part of the tree trunk, you may like to put the abbreviations SA (standing for sexual abuse) to symbolise that this has been a part of your history. I emphasise the word "part" here because SA is not "all" your history. Your history is and you are so much more than the SA. However, for this activity, this is the event that we are acknowledging.

    Now I invite you to add some fruit to the tree… The fruit represents the "new" thing that is unfolding in your life now and the new things that have emerged in your life over the last couple of years. You may like to write next to the fruit the name of the "new" thing that it represents.
6. As you look at your drawing, what does it communicate to you about:
    i) God
    ii) Yourself

    What feelings arise in you as you look at your drawing? For example: hope, peace, joy…

    How does your drawing change your perception of your healing journey? You may want to sum this up with one word on your drawing, for example, hope, transformation.

As you continue your healing journey, you may want to come back to this picture and keep adding to it the fruit of the "new things" that God is doing in you.

Allow it to remind you of the awesome grace that flows from the roots of God's love in your life, despite a traumatic history and may you keep experiencing how God's grace works through your history in the most beautiful way to produce "new" life within you.

Succeeding Gracefully

For as the rain and the snow come down from heaven,
and do not return there until they have watered the earth,
making it bring forth and sprout,
giving seed to the sower and bread to the eater,
so shall my word be that goes out from my mouth;
it shall not return to me empty;
but it shall accomplish that which I purpose;
and succeed in the thing for which I sent it.

Isaiah 55:10-11

ALL AROUND US, CREATION IS constantly echoing the marvellous cycle of life. If we quietly ponder it, we realise that everything it needs to flourish abundantly is so generously provided for. Creation does not exert effort to make it succeed; it succeeds through the grace that is gifted by life.

These beautiful verses from the Prophet Isaiah in the Hebrew Scriptures invite us to reflect on this and to discover the gift of God's grace that promises accomplishment and success in our life just as it achieves it in creation. The prophet here, as we have seen in previous chapters, is speaking God's word to a people in exile. God appeals through the prophet that "as the rain and snow" sent by God to give new life to the earth succeed, so shall God's promise to save Israel.

This verse so wonderfully describes the gift of God's life-giving grace that is poured out and multiplied. It is like "the rain and snow that come down from heaven": first, it waters the earth and seeps into its depths, there in hiding it continues to work in the silence and darkness, and eventually from the depths of the earth the seed sprouts into life rising up and breaking through the soil bringing forth new fruit visible to the eye, this fruit goes on to provide a harvest for the one who has worked to plant the seed, and the harvest provides nourishment for many people.

So not only does God's grace succeed in the tangible and visible, it also succeeds in things invisible to the human eye. You may not be aware, but every time you read God's Word in the Scriptures, God's grace: "rains" down in your heart, waters the ground of your being, seeps into the depths of your earth, and works silently and diligently in the cold and dark places within where you feel lifeless. In the same way that grace enables the tiny seeds in creation to break open and give birth to new life rising above and breaking through the soil, it does the same with the tiny seeds deep within us that break forth into new life and slowly rise to the surface, until the fruit comes forth and is visible in your life, whether it be more hope, more joy, more positivity, greater resilience, more courage. Each of us will gradually experience how grace is working within our life and succeeding gracefully.

Experiencing the Scripture in Creation

For this activity, you are invited to venture out into creation to a place that is sacred and life-giving for you. It may be a garden, a park or a reserve, or a mountain. When you arrive there, you are invited to take a walk, being mindful of the abundance of life in Creation. The steps below may help you to experience the Scripture while doing this.

1. Before you venture out, you may like to read the words of this Scripture slowly and attentively, being aware that God speaks to you and pours out grace through the Word in the Bible.
2. As you set out on your venture, try to hold on to the words of Scripture (Isaiah 55) in your heart.
3. When you reach your sacred place, begin to take a slow walk. As you walk notice creation around you… notice all the things that are propagating life around you: the trees, the flowers, the grass, the birds that are singing in the trees…

4. Now try to notice the detail in each of these things: for example, the abundance of leaves on a tree, the pattern on each leaf, the stem of a flower, the number of petals, the shapes of the petals....
5. Now try to imagine the life that went on beneath the soil that holds each of these things. You may like to imagine the process that went on in the depths of the dark and cold earth for this visible life to come to be.
6. Afterwards, you may like to spend time enjoying how such beautiful life sprang up from the invisible.
7. As you ponder the beauty of Creation around you, are you receiving something from it (For example: joy, pleasure, peace, inspiration, gratitude...)? This experience is a gift of God's grace to you through the visible.
8. As you continue to walk and enjoy your surroundings, you may like to recall the "new things" that you saw emerging in your life from the previous Chapter "Something New", that is, visible fruits of new life in you.
9. When you reflect on these "new things", what do they give you (i.e. joy, satisfaction...)?
10. These "new things" in you are not only the result of your work but they are also evidence of God's grace working in you. Are you able to identify how God's grace may have been working in the silence of your heart enabling these "new things" to emerge? (For example: through something you heard, read, something you or someone else did...). You may like to spend time appreciating this.
11. As you continue to walk and enjoy creation, you may like to imagine all the other "unnamed" seeds in the depths of your being that are waiting to break open. As you recall the words of Scripture, you are invited to believe that God is already pouring grace upon grace over these seeds and promises us that they will succeed in emerging to abundant new life.
12. Allow the Creation around you to confirm this truth for you through all the abundance of life that you see around you.

You may like to repeat this activity whenever you feel that you are not successful or that nothing is changing or happening within you. This activity helps to remind us that God's grace is always working in our life and doing something that will eventually break forth into life.

Rebuilding the Ruins

Your ancient ruins shall be rebuilt;
you shall raise up the foundations of many generations;
you shall be called the repairer of the breach,
the restorer of streets to live in.

Isaiah 58:12

ORIGINALLY, GOD CREATED US AS whole beings. As we saw in Genesis 2:7, God created a physical body from the earth and then God breathed spirit into it.[43] Through the gift of God's spirit the body received life so that humankind became a living being. From the time of creation, all human beings have a spiritual nature within a physical body. We are 'whole' beings and God has intricately interwoven each part of us in a marvellous way.[44] Paul alludes to wholeness in the first letter to the Corinthians where he talks about the body as being one although it is made up of many parts but we are created to function as a whole.[45]

God's greatest desire for us is to be whole, so much so, that when we are broken, God's heart aches and yearns for us to be restored to wholeness again. We can capture God's longing through this verse from the Prophet Isaiah. Remember, the people of Israel (to whom the prophet was directing these words) were a broken people with a history of a very broken past. Both personally, and as a people, they suffered huge losses. Everything that was familiar to them had been taken away from them and what was most precious to them, their temple of worship, had been totally destroyed and devastated. However, through the

---

43 Genesis 2:7
44 Psalm 139:14-15
45 1 Corinthians 12:12

prophet, God consoles the broken people of Israel and offers them the hope of restoration of their "ancient ruins".

Survivors of sexual abuse will easily identify with the brokenness of the people of Israel. We too are broken people who experience that our life is in "ruins" and who for decades, have been trying to pick up the broken pieces of our lives. Like the people of Israel, we too have suffered huge losses (and we could each make our lists) and we have also felt that what was most precious to us has been taken away from us leaving us devastated. We wonder in the silence of our hearts if restoration to wholeness will ever be possible again!

As God looks at us with great love and watches us grappling with our broken past, God longs for our wholeness. The words from this Scripture reflect this: "Your ancient ruins shall be rebuilt; you shall raise up the foundations of many generations; you shall be called the repairer of the breach." God does not want us to stay broken. God wants to repair us to wholeness again. God is very aware that our "ruins" are "ancient"; from a very long time ago but this is not an obstacle for God because when it comes to repairing God has no expiry time, time limit, or "repair by" date. Any time is good and right for God to begin, or to continue rebuilding and raising up our shattered foundations. All those parts of our life that have been "breached" and destroyed, God promises to repair into a dwelling that reflects wholeness.

If you live in a busy suburban area where there is some construction taking place, you might like to enjoy watching how it gradually comes together over time. It's a fascinating process to watch from the beginning, starting with the deep digging that is needed to lay the foundations, followed by laying the foundations and then building up on the foundations until the building is complete. In the initial process, there is a whole lot of dirt and dust and one could never imagine what will become of it all. When the building is finally finished there is awe at the beauty of the finished product as you remember that initial process of dirt and dust. Something wonderful has been raised up from the dirt.

God wants to also do this wonderful thing in our life too! Every time you see something being constructed around you, let it remind you of the rebuilding that God is doing with your "ancient ruins" and how your foundations are being raised up!

Experiencing the Scripture through visualisation and art
(Suggested materials: an A4 or A3 drawing book, crayons, paints or coloured pencils)

1. Read the words of this Scripture (Isaiah 58) slowly, being aware that God speaks to us when we read God's Word in the Bible[46].
2. You may like to divide your page in half by drawing a line down it
3. On the top of the left hand side you may like to write "Ancient Ruins"
4. On the left hand side, try to represent your "ancient ruins" by drawing some scattered individual bricks to represent all the things that the sexual abuse has "ruined" in you and your life. You may like to name each brick by writing inside it what it represents, for example, ability to speak out, mental health, ability to study, confidence… Draw and name as many bricks as you like.
5. On the top of right hand side, you may like to write "Rebuilding Ruins".

   Try to draw what "foundations being raised" looks like for you… whether it is slabs of concrete or piers… If you like, name what these foundations are for you, that is, the foundations you would like to be raised in your life (security, integrity, self-esteem…) On top of these foundations try to draw a brick wall (as if you were drawing a building) from the bricks that you have labelled on the left hand side of your page. Once you have drawn the brick wall, name your bricks individually on your brick wall.
6. As you look at your drawing, what does it communicate to you? You may want to sum this up in a few words written around your picture.

   What feelings arise in you as you look at your drawing? For example: hope, peace, joy…

---

[46] Documents of the Second Vatican Council, *Dei Verbum, Dogmatic Constitution on Divine Revelation*, #25.

How does your drawing change your perception of your healing journey?

7. You may want to draw some extra bricks or even like to finish your drawing by completing the building as you envisage it.

    As you continue healing, and are able to name other things that have been "ruined" in you, you may like to come back to this drawing and label the unlabelled bricks belonging to the wall on the right hand side.

Allow this picture to remind you of the work that God is doing in your life to restore you to wholeness.

Dry Bones Revived

The hand of the Lord came upon me, and he brought me out by the spirit of the Lord and set me down in the middle of a valley; it was full of bones. He led me all around them; there were very many lying in the valley, and they were very dry. He said to me, "Mortal, can these bones live?" I answered, "O Lord God, you know." Then he said to me, "Prophesy to these bones, and say to them: O dry bones, hear the word of the Lord. Thus says the Lord God to these bones: I will cause breath to enter you, and you shall live. I will lay sinews on you, and will cause flesh to come upon you, and cover you with skin, and put breath in you, and you shall live; and you shall know that I am the Lord."

So I prophesied as I had been commanded; and as I prophesied, suddenly there was a noise, a rattling, and the bones came together, bone to its bone. I looked, and there were sinews on them, and flesh had come upon them, and skin had covered them; but there was no breath in them. Then he said to me, "Prophesy to the breath, prophesy, mortal, and say to the breath: Thus says the Lord God: Come from the four winds, O breath, and breathe upon these slain, that they may live." I prophesied as he commanded me, and the breath came into them, and they lived, and stood on their feet, a vast multitude.

Ezekiel 37:1-10

HAVE YOU EVER WOKEN UP from a very vivid and disturbing dream and thought to yourself, "I wonder what it could mean!" We can imagine that when the exiled people of Israel listened to this very eerie yet vivid vision expressed through the prophet Ezekiel, they too thought to themselves, 'what does this vision mean for us?'[47] Ezekiel's vision of the dry bones is truly astonishing and suggests that what is dead (in the context of these verses, "spiritually" dead), referring in this case to the exiled people of Israel, might live again.

In the beginning, the vision that the prophet presents to the people speaks of death and hopelessness but it is slowly transformed into life and hope. After being "set down" into a "valley full of dry bones" and being "led all around them", God asks the prophet, "can these bones live?" One would expect the most logical human response would be, "of course these bones can't live! They are so dry that they have been well and truly dead for a long time and never to live again!" The prophet, however, gives God the benefit of the doubt replying, "O, Lord God, you know." Then God asks the prophet to "prophesy to these dead bones and say to them: O dry bones, hear the word of the Lord."

The "dry bones" refers to the people of Israel.[48] At "hearing the word of the Lord", God promises the people that, "I will cause breath to enter you, and you shall live."

In this slow process of coming back to life, God promises to restore what has been torn away, to cover up what is vulnerable and exposed, and, finally, to give back life; "I will lay sinews on you, and will cause flesh to come upon you, and cover you with skin, and put breath in you, and you shall live; and you shall know that I am the Lord."

So as the prophet prophesied, it happens just as God promises; "suddenly there was a noise, a rattling, and the bones came together, bone to its bone. I looked, and there were sinews on them, and flesh had come upon them, and skin had covered them" but "there was no breath in them". The prophet is then commanded by God to prophesy to "the breath" and as the prophet does, "the

---

47 Ezekiel prophesied from 593-571BCE and travelled between Mesopotamia and Syro-Palestine. He was a vigorous religious thinker of his time, and as the book of the prophet discloses, he saw strange visions.
48 Ezekiel 37:11

breath came into them, and they lived, and stood on their feet, a vast multitude."

In the vision of the prophet, the "breath" refers to the "spirit".[49] It is the same "breath" that God breathed into humankind created from dust.[50] Just as the "breath" gave life to humankind at its origins, this "breath" also gives life when we experience spiritual death, as did the people of Israel in exile. The imagery of seeing the people living and standing on their feet as a vast multitude is indeed a very hopeful one. It is an image that expresses God as a God of Life and the One who gives all Life through "breath"; a "breath" that is able to restore and revive all from the power of spiritual death.

For survivors, as well as for those who have not experienced sexual abuse, there are times in our life journey where we feel "spiritually" dead and this is a normal part of our human experience. There are many events that can trigger it: a traumatic experience, an accident, loss of a loved one, a break in a relationship, a physical or mental illness, an unhealthy lifestyle, a humiliation, loss of employment…

Whatever the event may be, we are left feeling that all our hopes and dreams for the future have been cruelly torn away from us, killing our joy, our enthusiasm and passion for life, our motivation, our confidence, our faith, our trust in the supreme good… We feel exposed, vulnerable and dead. Our heart feels the lifeless weight of death and it seems like nothing at all can possibly stir our numb and stony heart! Although we are physically breathing and moving externally, we feel spiritually asphyxiated and dead within. It is as though all life has been sucked out of every single bone in our body and all that remains is a body of two hundred and six dry bones. We feel powerless to change our situation and circumstances.

Through this Scripture, God promises to restore us to life by "hearing the word of the Lord". We "hear the word of the Lord" when we read and engage with the Scriptures and as we receive God's words into our heart, we receive

---

49 Ezekiel 36:26-27a "A new heart I will give you, and a new spirit I will put within you; and I will remove from your body the heart of stone and give you a heart of flesh. I will put my spirit within you."
50 Genesis 2:7 "Then the Lord God formed man from the dust of the ground."

"Spirit" and "Life".[51] Jesus reminds his disciples of this in the gospel of John as they go through a very challenging time and are tempted to give up. Jesus says to them, "The Spirit alone gives life. Human effort accomplishes nothing. And the very words I have spoken to you are spirit and life."[52] The action of reading God's words, engaging with God, and receiving Spirit and Life from God is what we call prayer.

The Spirit of God that we receive as we pray with the Scriptures is not silent, it makes "a noise" and causes "a rattling" within ourselves as we begin to experience movements, sometimes subtle, sometimes more obvious; sadness slowly dissipating, discouragement scampering as new courage emerges, hopelessness fading as hope rises, and doubts evaporating as renewed faith rains upon us ... Sometimes it is the "noise" of intuition, a heartfelt stirring to either do or confront something that we believe will be good for ourselves or others, or to stop doing or pursuing something or that may be harming ourselves or others. It is like we hear within ourselves the subtle sound of distant music until eventually; we experience the gift of being restored spiritually to Life through the "breath", that is, through the Spirit that we receive through the Scriptures. Like the people of Israel, the gift of renewed life empowers us to stand and continue our journey forward.

So whenever we feel spiritually dead, God promises us that the gift of Life is not far away. It is within our reach through the Scriptures and we receive it by reading and engaging with God through the Scriptures.

Although this vision of the prophet Ezekiel is a very ancient one; one that on first reading can be frightening, it is still full of meaning for us today and holds within it the secret to and of Life. As you continue to engage with the Scripture through this book, hopefully, you too will come to experience it within your own being as your "dry bones" live again!

---

51 Documents of the Second Vatican Council, *Dei Verbum, Dogmatic Constitution on Divine Revelation*, #25.
52 John 6:63

Experiencing the Scripture through visualisation and art
(Suggested materials: an A4 or A3 drawing book, crayons, paints or coloured pencils)

1. Read the words of this Scripture (Ezekiel 37) slowly, being aware that God speaks to us when we read God's Word in the Bible.[53] We refer to this as prayer.
2. You may like to title your page: "Dry Bones".
3. Draw what this "valley of dry bones" looks like for you.
4. Can you name what has/is draining life from your bones? You may like to write this around the "dry bones" you have drawn on your page.
5. Can you name the hopes and dreams that you feel have been torn away from you? You may like to write this in "the valley of bones" that you have drawn.
6. Can you name how this has left you feeling (for example discouraged, sad, confused….). You may like to write these feelings somewhere in your valley.
7. As you look at what you have drawn, listen to God saying to you through the Scripture, ": O dry bones of _____ (put your name here), hear the word of the Lord… I will cause breath to enter you, and you shall live… I will put breath in you, and you shall live…" Reread these words several times with the awareness that it is God speaking to you. Allow them to sink into your heart.
8. As you listen to these words from God, what are you experiencing? Can you identify a "noise" or a "rattling" of the Spirit slowly breathing life within you?
9. How do you experience this being manifested? For example, is it a rattling of an intuition, or a movement of some negative feeling to a more positive one, or something else?

---

[53] Documents of the Second Vatican Council, *Dei Verbum, Dogmatic Constitution on Divine Revelation*, #25.

10. Try to portray in your drawing what this "noise" or "rattling" of the Spirit looks like as it enters your "valley of dry bones".
11. As you look at your drawing, what does it communicate to you about God? You may want to sum this up in one or two words on your picture.
12. How does your drawing change your perception of your healing journey?

Next time you feel like you are in a "valley of dry bones", you may find it helpful to come back to your picture. Read the words of this Scripture (Ezekiel 37) slowly and reflectively as you look at your drawing and allow God to breathe Spirit and Life in you again.

Life-Giving Reservoirs

The man brought me back to the entrance to the temple, and I saw water coming out from under the threshold of the temple toward the east (for the temple faced east). The water was coming down from under the south side of the temple, south of the altar. He then brought me out through the north gate and led me around the outside to the outer gate facing east, and the water was trickling from the south side. As the man went eastward with a measuring line in his hand, he measured off a thousand cubits and then led me through water that was ankle-deep. He measured off another thousand cubits and led me through water that was knee-deep. He measured off another thousand and led me through water that was up to the waist. He measured off another thousand, but now it was a river that I could not cross, because the water had risen and was deep enough to swim in—a river that no one could cross. He asked me, "Son of man, do you see this?" Then he led me back to the bank of the river. When I arrived there, I saw a great number of trees on each side of the river. He said to me, "This water flows toward the eastern region and goes down into the Arabah, where it enters the Dead Sea. When it empties into the sea, the salty water there becomes fresh. Swarms of living creatures will live wherever the river flows. There will be large numbers of fish, because this water flows there and makes the salt water fresh; so where the river flows everything will live. Fishermen will stand along the shore; from En Gedi to En Eglaim there will be places for spreading nets. The fish will be of many kinds—like the fish of the Mediterranean Sea. But the swamps and marshes will not become fresh; they will be left for salt. Fruit trees of all kinds will grow on both banks of the river. Their leaves will not wither, nor will their fruit fail. Every month they will bear fruit, because the water from the sanctuary flows to them. Their fruit will serve for food and their leaves for healing."

Ezekiel 47:1-12

READING THIS SCRIPTURE REMINDED ME of a story I once heard. One day, a man ventured out on his boat and on his way back, when he was still a long way off from the shore, he ran out of petrol. He spent a couple of days in the water drifting along in his boat. He had no food and water supplies and was slowly becoming delirious. He was so tempted to drink the salt water but knew the consequences could be fatal, so he hung on hoping that someone would find him very soon. Just when the man was losing all hope of being saved, a helicopter flew over and rescued him. As soon as he was air lifted into the helicopter, he asked his rescuer, "Do you have some water? I am so thirsty!" The rescuer replied, "How is that? Didn't you know that you were floating on fresh water!" The man looked at him in disbelief. He was sitting on a reservoir of fresh drinking water and he didn't realise it! There he was, literally dying of thirst yet he had a whole supply of fresh water right at his fingertips.

This Scripture speak to us of life-giving waters that flow from the sacred temple. The image of water is associated with God's divine presence[54] and the river imagery resonates with the Creation story where God's garden is a watery and fertile place[55]. The man in this story shows Ezekiel a stream that is flowing out from beneath the temple and out under the exterior east gate. Leading

---

54 Ezekiel 1:24; Ezekiel 43:2
55 Genesis 2:10 "A river watering the garden flowed from Eden; from there it was separated into four headwaters."

Ezekiel into the stream, he takes four measurements revealing that the river is growing progressively larger and deeper – first *ankle deep*, then *knee deep*, then *up to the waist*, and finally *could not be crossed*. Retracing their steps, Ezekiel notices the fertile growth on the riverbank *of fruit trees of all kinds*. The man explains to Ezekiel that the river of water flows into the Dead Sea where the salty sea water becomes fresh water making it possible for all living creatures to live and swarms of fish to exist in large numbers. For the same reason, even on the river banks, fruit trees of all kinds will grow, their leaves never withering, and always bearing fruit because the water from the sanctuary flows to them which is why the fruit from the trees will serve for food and their leaves for healing.

So how is this story relevant to our story as survivors of sexual abuse?

In the Chapter titled "Divinely Loved", we saw how we *are* God's Temple – *the place where God lives and loves us divinely*. In the same way that life-giving water flowed from the sacred temple, progressively becoming larger and deeper until it became a river, it also flows from within our sacred dwelling progressively welling up to become a larger and deeper spring of water and, in the same way that the water turned the salty waters of the Dead Sea into fresh water where swarms of fish could live and multiply, and trees on the banks of the river could be eternally fruitful producing food and medicine, so too will the deep spring of fresh water that wells up from deep within us. As this water of God flows into our own "Dead Sea", everything within us and without will be enlivened, and new life within us will flourish and grow. Like the trees on the riverbank of all kinds that bore eternal fruit, our life too will be eternally fruitful because of the life-giving waters that flow from our inner sanctuary.

So we can be like the man I mentioned at the beginning of this chapter who was stranded on his boat and nearly dying of thirst without realizing that he was sitting on a reservoir of fresh drinking water. Too often in life, we are spiritually *dying of thirst* and starved of fresh drinking water particularly as we go through our healing process. We thirst for all sorts of things: love, truth, acceptance, justice, peace, understanding, courage, strength, soothing, joy, faith, freedom… We go in search of quenching our thirst, perhaps in people, in therapies, in systems, in communities, in hobbies but we are not satisfied. During all the time we are searching, we do not realise that we are sitting on a reservoir of life-giving drinking water. We are waiting to be saved by someone or something that can quench our thirst but not realizing that what we are searching for is within our reach; it is within us.

Imagine having eternity right at your fingertips and not even knowing it! This is what it is like when we do not realise that we have an eternal source of life-giving water within ourselves. All too often, this appears to be the reality our life that is reflected when we fail to quench and satisfy our spiritual thirst. Jesus perceived this and he did not want the truth that we are sitting on life-giving reservoirs to remain the world's best kept secret. Jesus wanted everyone to know how to access this reservoir which is why in the gospel of John, at a very crowded Jewish Festival he cries out, "If anyone thirsts, let him come to me and drink. Whoever believes in me, as the Scripture has said, 'Out of his heart will flow rivers of living water.'"[56]

We receive the same invitation from God through the words from the Prophet Ezekiel; to believe that flowing from our own inner sanctuary - the place where God lives - is a river of life-giving water that has the capacity to quench everything we thirst for in life. Yes, we are sitting on a life-giving reservoir and we have eternity at our fingertips.

So next time we are spiritually thirsty and trying to quench our thirst in places that leave us dissatisfied, let's drink from our own life-giving reservoir and experience how it enlivens our "Dead Sea", making new life grow and blossom both within us and without, quenching our deepest thirst.

Experiencing the Scripture through visualisation and art
(Suggested materials: an A4 or A3 drawing book, crayons, paints or coloured pencils)

1. Read the words of this Scripture (Ezekiel 47) slowly, being aware that God speaks to us when we read God's Word in the Bible.[57]

---

56 Ref John 7:37-38
57 Documents of the Second Vatican Council, Dei Verbum, Dogmatic Constitution on Divine Revelation, #25.

2. You may like to title your page: "Life-Giving Reservoirs".
3. You may like to draw a huge heart on your page representing your own heart.
4. Within your heart you may want to draw what you imagine your life-giving reservoir looks like. Within your drawing, you may want to capture the life-giving water of God flowing into your "Dead Sea".

    You may like to see your "Dead Sea" as all the things you are spiritually thirsting for (for example: acceptance, understanding…) You may want to name these things around the sea you have drawn.
5. You may like to also imagine the life-giving water of God flowing outside your heart, into your: relationships, work, hobbies… What sorts of things do you imagine blossoming or growing from this "life-giving" water (joy, confidence)? You may want to name some things and write it in the water flowing outside your heart.
6. As you look at your drawing, what does it communicate to you? You may want to sum this up in a few words written around your picture.
7. What feelings arise in you as you look at your drawing? For example, hope, peace, joy…
8. How does your drawing change your perception of your healing journey?

Whenever you are thirsting for life, come back to this picture and let it remind you of the life-giving reservoir you have within.

*"I can be changed by what happens to me.
But I refuse to be reduced by it."*
Maya Angelou

PART II

Coming Forward In Our New Self

(This part deals with confronting issues that prevent us from moving forward in life.)

Coming Forward - Leaving the hidden life behind

EVERY SURVIVOR OF CHILDHOOD SEXUAL abuse knows what it is to live a "hidden" life. Not only did our perpetrator(s) force us to hide the sexual abuse but we were also forced to hide any details associated with it: where we were taken or planned to be taken, the activities we did during those times, the personal things that were revealed to us … Our perpetrator(s) even coerced us to tell lies if we were questioned and to hide the truth. Consequently, from a young age we were groomed by our perpetrator(s) to live a "hidden" life and to hold in our heart the heavy weight of secrets; destructive secrets that no child should ever have to hold.

Sadly, by the time we were teenagers, we were very well practised at living a life of secrets and lies; it became the norm for us. Tragically, as the years go on and we continue to live this norm, our true identity gets buried so deeply within ourselves that we become disconnected from the truth of who we really are. Undeniably, being disconnected from our true identity has profound detrimental spiritual effects on us; life loses meaning and purpose and we feel lost.

As life graciously unfolds, we are presented with opportunities to come forward with our truth and to step out of the hidden life that we have lived for so long. For survivors of sexual abuse, coming forward with our truth is the key to re-connecting to our true identity. It is a step that requires boldness and, if taken, spiritual healing begins to happen.

You may find the following Scripture reading helpful to identify the events in your life that have or are inviting you to come forward with your truth and to leave your hidden life behind.

The Scripture Reading

In those days Jesus came from Nazareth of Galilee and was baptised by John in the Jordan. And just as he was coming up out of the water, he saw the heavens torn apart and the Spirit descending like a dove on him. And a voice came from heaven, "You are my Son, the Beloved; with you I am well pleased."

Mark 1:9-11

Jesus' baptism was a very significant event. It marked the end of Jesus' "hidden" life and the initiation of his public ministry.

The "hidden" life of Jesus refers to the period of his life lived in Nazareth from the age of 12 up to the beginning of his public ministry. These years formed the foundation for Jesus' public ministry because during them he grew in wisdom and grace[58]. What remained "hidden" during this period was Jesus' true identity and who he really was - the Son of God, the Messiah.

Jesus' baptism marks a new stage in his life. It is a moment of grace where Jesus listens to God affirming his true identity, "You are my Son, the Beloved, with whom I am well pleased". The affirmation of Jesus' true identity fills him with purpose and meaning and through his baptism he is empowered by the Holy Spirit and comes forward in readiness to initiate his ministry which will involve publicly revealing his true identity.

So how is this meaningful for survivors of sexual abuse? As life unfolds for us, so do events where we feel invited to leave behind the "hidden" life that we are living and to reveal the deeper truth about ourselves.[59] I refer to these events as "baptisms" of the Holy Spirit; moments of intense grace where we experience the Holy Spirit affirming our truth in our heart and empowering us to come forward to reveal it.

Often these events can take us by surprise and stir us profoundly. They can be as simple as reading a newspaper article or hearing a radio interview

---

[58] Luke 2:52 "And Jesus grew in wisdom and stature, and in favour with God and people."

[59] Sexual abuse is a sensitive issue. It is deeply personal and intimate and not everyone needs to know about it. Choosing who to reveal our truth to calls for discernment and it is important that we feel safe when we are revealing our truth. Revealing our truth may be in the form of seeing a psychologist, confronting the institution responsible, telling the truth to our family, joining a survivor's support group.

about the topic of sexual abuse and as we are reading or hearing it, we are saying to ourselves, "Yes, I know what they are talking about! That's me! That's my truth! That happened to me!" Through that article or interview our own truth is being affirmed and we feel empowered or invited to come forward to reveal our truth. As we do, we begin to heal spiritually as we reconnect to our own truth.

Not only do these "baptisms of the Holy Spirit" reconnect us to our own truth but they affirm in us a truth that is even greater than our own – that we are children of God, loved by God and with whom God is "well pleased". Baptisms of the Holy Spirit affirm us in our deepest identity. The truth of who we are for God holds our truth, meaning that although we are survivors of sexual abuse, we are much more than this; we are a child of God, loved by God and God is "well pleased" with us. Standing in the greater truth of who we are for God empowers us to come forward to reveal our own truth. It restores spiritual purpose and meaning to our life.

So let's try to be attentive to the baptism of the Holy Spirit events in our life when they appear for they will gift us with spiritual healing.

Experiencing the Scripture through prayer, visualisation and art
(Suggested materials: an A4 or A3 drawing book, crayons, paints or coloured pencils)

1. On a fresh page, you may like to put the title: "Come Forward – Leaving behind the "hidden" life.
2. Read the Scripture reading of Mark 1:9-11 slowly and try to visualise the scene.
3. Attempt to colourfully draw what you have visualised. (Remember, it is not about drawing perfectly but rather giving expression to what you experience as you read the Scripture.)
4. Imagine what Jesus may have been feeling and/or experiencing as the Spirit descends on him and God affirms "You are my Son, my Beloved, with whom I am well pleased".
5. Take some time now to reflect on your picture. It is a scene full of grace. Imagine that it is about you, that is, it is your baptism.

Visualise that it is you coming up from the water, the heavens are opening above you, the Spirit is descending upon you and your truth is being affirmed.

6. Can you identify events in your life that have been moments of intense grace where your truth – "I am a survivor of sexual abuse" – has been affirmed (for example: the mention of sexual abuse in the media, in the work-place, or at a conference or retreat, listening to a survivor's story…).

These events are baptisms of the Spirit in the sense that through them the Holy Spirit is deeply stirring our heart and reminding us of our truth. They are enlightening and empowering events where heaven opens from within us and reconnects us to our truth.

7. Did these events invite you in any way to come forward and leave your "hidden" life behind, that is, to reveal your truth?

How did you come forward with your truth (for example: spoke to a trained professional or someone you could trust, confronted the responsible institution)?

If you came forward, how did it feel not having to hide your truth? How did you experience a sense of spiritual healing (for example: a greater sense of freedom, reconnection with self…)?

You may like to express this in words on your drawing.

8. As you absorb your picture, try also to absorb God's words in your heart "X (put your name here), you are my son/daughter, my Beloved, with whom I am well pleased"[60].

---

[60] This phrase may stir up traumatic memories associated with the perpetrator so I will leave it to the survivor to discern if they feel up to continuing with this activity or not. In the event that you would like to continue the activity and experience painful memories or flashbacks, you may find that working through the following steps is helpful in overcoming some of the spiritual impacts that the sexual abuse has had on your relating to God: 1. Was there a particular thought that came to your mind or did you experience a flashback? 2. As this came to you, what were you feeling? (Anxiety, fear, terror…) 3. Try to identify who these thoughts, flashbacks, or feelings refer to? (For example, your perpetrator) 4. Once you have identified who your responses refer to, try to be aware that now you are in the presence of God who is Love and not in the presence of your perpetrator. Some self-talk may be helpful, for example, "I am safe! I am not with my perpetrator. I am with God who is Love. God is not my perpetrator or like my perpetrator. God and my perpetrator are very different." 5. Try to silence all the noises in your heart and let God assure you "I am God and I am not your perpetrator!" 6. If you feel calm enough, you may want to proceed with the activity.

9. As you listen to God's Word in your heart, what do you experience (i.e. courage, strength, acceptance, motivation)?
10. As you look at your picture, and acknowledge the baptisms of the Holy Spirit in your life, how do you feel?
    How is your picture inviting you to receive future baptisms of the Holy Spirit?

The next time you experience a baptism of the Holy Spirit, you may like to come back to this drawing and allow God to speak to you through it.

The Scripture experienced in my life

One day while working, I received a phone call from a radio presenter who was very eager to interview me about my first book *Child, Arise! The Courage to Stand. A Spiritual Handbook for Survivors of Sexual Abuse* which had been awarded the 2016 Australian Christian Book of the Year. As I listened to him, my heart was pounding so hard against my chest that I thought it was going to jump out!

Surviving sexual abuse is something that I have shared with only a handful of people but after winning the Award I was being invited to come forward publicly to talk about my book. Clearly, the event of winning the award was a baptism of the Holy Spirit for me. Up until then, the completion of my book was a private matter. When, however, I received my award publicly, it was for me the first time I ever stood before an unknown audience of people as a survivor of sexual abuse. It was a moment of intense grace and, as I stood publicly in my own truth, I felt God affirming in me the greatest truth that I can ever know – I am God's child, God's beloved, and God is pleased with me. I recognise the experience was a pure gift of God's grace.

Through the radio presenter's request for an interview, I was being invited to a further baptism of the Holy Spirit. I accepted the invitation to do the radio interview, although I felt anxious about it. Again, it was a moment of intense grace and as I finished the interview it was as if heaven opened up from within my heart and God affirmed in me that I am so much more to him than a survivor of sexual abuse. I am God's child, God's beloved and God is very pleased with me no matter how or what I feel or think.

It was never in my plans to reveal my truth so publicly but the events of life were now inviting me to come forward in my truth and to leave my "hidden" life behind. As I do come forward in my truth, not only do I experience the gift of spiritual healing through reconnecting with myself but I also experience that my deepest identity and who I am for God is constantly being affirmed.

I now realise that the baptismal events of the Holy Spirit empower us to live out our purpose and give meaning to our life. So may we recognise and welcome them when they come!

Your experience of Scripture through prayer, visualisation and art

You may like to take some time to journal about how you have experienced this Scripture reading through art and what it has conveyed to you about your own personal journey. This may be helpful to refer back to in the future.

Having a Voice

SILENCE, PARTICULARLY LONG PERIODS OF silence, may be an issue for survivors of sexual abuse. I observed this in my former ministry while facilitating weekend and week-long silent retreats. Most people would gently ease into the silent atmosphere but more than often there always seemed to be one or two who would really struggle to enter the silence even though these people genuinely desired to do the retreat. It was not uncommon, when listening to these people's story to discover a history of childhood sexual abuse.

Through my own experience of doing silent retreats, I came to the realisation that silence – especially if it is imposed, requested, or demanded of us – may be a language that we associate with our past traumatic experiences. The first silent retreat I ever did was for one month. I recall how terrified and anxious I was as we began the retreat. Although the physical place I was in was safe, the silence made me feel unsafe and uneasy. I spent the first week resisting the silence and looking for opportunities to talk with people and break the silence. I remember going out into the bush and singing at the top of my voice just to hear the sound of music. The silence felt tortuous. As I looked at those around me seemingly enjoying the silence, I never knew why it was not so for me. It wasn't until several years later when I began my healing journey that I made the connection and understood for the first time that for survivors of sexual abuse, silence is a language that we associate with our traumatic memories.

Silence was forced upon us during the time of the sexual abuse by our perpetrator(s). We were constantly forced to "Be quiet!" and "Don't tell anyone or else…" The "or else" were threats! Afraid for our safety, we kept silent but meanwhile we lived in constant terror as the abuse continued. Often our perpetrators would interrogate us to make sure that we didn't reveal the secret. It was drummed into us that silence was for the better because "no one is going to believe you", they will say, "you are a liar", and "you are bad", and "they will be angry with you".

Being silent meant that we did not have a voice[61] and that we never had the opportunity to hear our own voice. Consequently, we never learnt to speak out! The effects of remaining silent and not speaking out when situations call us to, can bring us to experience further harm in the future of being re-victimised.

Learning to break the silence and have a voice is not only vital for our own healing but also to prevent situations of further abuse in the future.

Although there are many Scripture readings that invite us into a healthy prayerful silence where we are nurtured and soothed, there are also many Scripture readings that invite us to have a voice and speak out. God never intended for us to be silent creatures. For just as the birds sing their song throughout the day, we too are invited to let others hear our voice as we speak out the truth in love. The Scripture below is a beautiful example of this.

The Scripture Reading

Therefore whatever has been said in the dark will be heard in the light, and what has been whispered behind closed doors will be proclaimed from the housetops.

Luke 12:3

In the biblical context, this Scripture reading comes immediately after Jesus has spoken out against the hypocritical behaviours of the Scribes and Pharisees. Jesus is speaking here to a crowd of disciples in the "thousands".

Jesus shows us through his life what it means to have a voice and speak out. Jesus didn't settle for any "unhealthy" silence in his life. When he noticed something was not right, he spoke the truth and brought it out into the open! Jesus was not afraid to publicly denounce what was covered up and harmful to others, particularly when it was coming from the religious leaders of his time. This emphasises that Jesus was someone who loved truth and integrity. By speaking out, he called those in authority to be responsible and accountable for their actions and inactions. This infuriated those concerned who tried to silence him but Jesus not being intimated by them, continued to speak out. Eventually, Jesus paid with his life the cost of speaking the truth.

---

61 Having a voice refers to being able to speak our truth safely and express our needs and wants.

Just as Jesus saw what wasn't right with the religious system and leaders of his time, God sees what isn't right with the religious and government institutions of our time, but, more importantly, God sees the wrong and injustice that has been done to us, and for some, done within a religious institution.

In this Scripture verse, Jesus encourages us not to be afraid to break the decades long silence and reveal the truth of what has happened or happens to us "in the dark" and "behind closed doors". Jesus never asks us to silence the truth especially when a wrong or injustice has been done. On the contrary, he urges us to do as he did – speak out – and bring the truth out into the open so that further harm is prevented to ourselves or any other person.

It is, however, important to clarify what Jesus means by "… proclaimed from the housetops". This is not meant to be taken literally and that we go to a housetop and proclaim that we have been sexually abused. Sexual abuse is a sensitive issue and it needs to be treated with sensitivity and delicacy. What has happened to us is deeply personal and intimate and not everyone needs to know about it. Choosing to whom we will reveal it requires discernment and discretion; and creating boundaries for ourselves to feel safe is important when it comes to revealing our story. In fact, many survivors may chooseto share their story with only a small number of people over a life time and even then, there may be certain details of their story that they choose never to reveal. What Jesus is highlighting when he says "… proclaim from the housetops" is letting the/our truth come out so that whatever is wrong can be addressed and a process of change can begin to happen.

Institutions will only change wrongs that are being concealed when people are bold enough to come forward and speak the truth. When we hear the voices of multitudes of people speaking out, it is a powerful stimulus, not only calling for change but generating it. We witnessed this occurring during the process of the Royal Commission into Institutional Responses to Child Sexual Abuse in Australia (2012-2017).

But not only does speaking out instigate change, it is also essential for our personal healing journey. Speaking out is like choosing to open up the doors of a very dark room that has for decades been tightly bolted and smells of death and letting the light come in to gradually light up every nook and cranny.

Initially, the revelation is shocking and can leave a disturbing impression on the mind of those who hear it. Eventually, though, the light brings with it a sense of freedom as it enables the room finally to be emptied out, cleaned and aired, allowing a bigger living space from within. Speaking out and having a voice is key to creating new possibilities in our own story.

May Jesus' words in this Scripture continue to inspire and encourage us when opportunities present and call us to have a voice and speak out.

Experiencing the Scripture through prayer, visualisation and art
(Suggested materials: an A4 or A3 drawing book, crayons, paints or coloured pencils)

1. On a fresh page you may like to put the title: "Having a Voice – Speaking Out".
2. Read the Scripture verse of Luke 12:3 slowly and try to absorb the words.
3. On your page, draw the profile image of a face with an open mouth which symbolises breaking the silence (remember, it's not about having a perfect image).
4. Try to visualise that the image you have drawn is you breaking your silence. What are the silences you have broken in your life and proclaimed in the light (they may have been related to your past, family related, work related, community related)?
5. You may like to write these things coming out of the open mouth on the picture you have drawn.
6. Can you recall how you felt after telling the truth?
7. Did telling the truth come with a personal cost for you (i.e. to your physical, mental, psychological, spiritual well-being, your family, work…)
8. In hindsight, what do you see have been the benefits of speaking out?
9. Being mindful of the life of Jesus, do you see resemblances in your

experience and from what you know of the life of Jesus?
10. Are there "other" silences in your life that you would like to break? Can you name them?
11. Keeping these in mind, read the words of Jesus again, allowing them to empower you to have a voice and speak out?
12. Looking at your picture, try to visualise that you are breaking these silences and speaking out? You may like to write these ones in a different colour to the others on your drawing.
13. How does this make you feel?
14. What would enable you to pursue this? (i.e. having support, wellness of physical health…)
15. You may like to set yourself some goals to work towards "breaking" these "silences".
    On the back of your drawing, you may like to draw a heading "Goals" and then to list your goals.
16. Keep trying to progress in these goals as a way of working towards having a voice and speaking out.
17. When you feel your "silences" haunting you, you may like to come back to this Scripture reading and allow it to remind you of what you saw at the light of your reflection on Scripture today.

The Scripture experienced in my life

Some days after I prayed this Scripture, I was listening to a talk given by a priest who was talking about scenarios where the Church was being persecuted for her stand on moral issues. One of the issues he touched on was sexual abuse in the Church. Although he acknowledged that it is a scandal, he presented the Royal Commission into Institutional Responses to Childhood Sexual Abuse as persecuting the Catholic Church particularly with the constant interrogation of Cardinal George Pell. His view was that sexual abuse was happening in other non-religious organisations but they weren't being targeted as hard as the Church was. He deepened on his view point.

By the end of his talk, I was so distressed and angered that I felt I could not simply leave and remain silent. I felt the Holy Spirit urging me to speak out and have my voice heard. I had a strong sense that if I held my silence and walked away, I was only perpetuating the impacts of the trauma for myself. I realised that this was another opportunity to break my silence and I chose to do it. I was aware of the importance of not being reactive in my approach but rather to respond to what this priest had said by sharing my truth.

I presented myself to the priest as a survivor of sexual abuse by a member of the clergy and told him that I would like to express what it was like being at the other end of the issue he was talking about. I shared my view that there is a difference between "persecution" and being held accountable for wrong that has been done particularly when it has caused grave harm. I expressed that in my case, there is evidence that what happened to me was a result of the Church not acting responsibly when it had been warned of potential danger of appointing my perpetrator to a parish. In my case, the Church had failed in responsibility and consequently, I am a casualty who now needs to deal with the ongoing impacts and effects of the trauma suffered decades ago. I expressed how disappointed I was that the Church, up until the present, had not yet apologised for the grave harm done. I questioned the integrity of the message of the Love of Christ that the Church preaches. How could the Church demand that I love with Christ's love when he has not given me an example of Christ's love by acknowledging the grave harm that has been done?[62] The response I got was silence.

I can't forget the freedom I experienced from speaking out and having my voice heard rather than walking away in silence. I did think about how the priest may have felt after hearing my story and my hope is that through it, he was able to reflect on this issue in a very different way and that in the future his own views may change around this issue so that if he does speak about it publicly, he will express a view that is more truthful and that expresses the integrity of Christ's love for those who have survived sexual abuse.

---

62 It is important for me to acknowledge that when I refer to the Church, I am not referring to all members of the clergy but rather to those in leadership whose responsibility it is to respond to survivors and the issue of sexual abuse with truth, justice and integrity. During my former ministry, and in the present, I know there exist priests who live out the message of Christ's love with integrity.

Your experience of Scripture through prayer, visualisation and art

You may like to take some time to journal about how you have experienced this Scripture reading through art and what it has conveyed to you about your own personal journey. This may be helpful to refer back to in the future.

Saying "No"

THE WORD "NO" SEEMS SMALL but when we say it to mark a boundary, its effect on our well-being is huge.

Personal boundaries are the physical, emotional and mental and spiritual limits that we create to identify what are reasonable, safe and permissible ways for others to behave around us and how we will respond when someone steps outside those limits. Personal boundaries guard and protect the dignity of our person and protect us from being manipulated, used or violated by others. They enable us to separate who we are, and what we think and feel, from the thoughts and feelings of others and express "I am me. I am not you. We are different."

We are not born knowing personal boundaries. They are something that we need to be taught from an early age and continue to develop as we grow into adulthood.

Sadly, personal boundaries are not always respected. In children who have been sexually abused, personal boundaries have been disrespected and broken at all levels – physically, mentally, emotionally, spiritually, and psychologically – affecting the most sacred part of the dignity of the person.

Consequently, survivors of sexual abuse struggle to re-establish boundaries as we grow into adulthood. As a child, the lines that marked a limit to make us feel protected were erased by the intrusion of our perpetrator leaving us dangerously vulnerable to repeated abuse. Re-establishing healthy boundaries is the key to preventing this.

The most fundamental boundary is the right to say "no". Saying yes to everything means lacking personal boundaries. Saying "no" allows us to define our space and put our well-being at heart. "No!" also enables us to take back power and control over our own lives when someone else holds it.

Daring to set boundaries by saying "no" is about having the courage to love ourselves, even when we risk disappointing others. Our real worth is not based on if others approve of us or not. Our worthiness comes from our deepest identity revealing who we truly are – a son and daughter created and loved by God! Only when we believe, deep down, that we *are* enough can we say "Enough!"

Positively, saying "no" is vital for the health and healing of survivors of sexual abuse.

When we look at the life of Jesus in the Scriptures, we notice that he was very good at practising boundaries in his personal life and also in his work and ministry.

The Scripture Reading

At daybreak he departed and went into a deserted place. And the crowds were looking for him; and when they reached him, they wanted to prevent him from leaving them. Be he said to them, "I must proclaim the good news of the kingdom of God to the other cities also; for I was sent for this purpose." So he continued proclaiming the message in the synagogues of Judea.

Luke 4:42-44

The events of the evening prior to this Scripture (Luke 4:38-42) are significant and help us to understand the boundaries Jesus establishes.

Jesus was visiting Simon's mother-in-law. He wakes up early after a very busy evening, curing not only Simon's mother-in-law but many people who were brought to him with various kinds of diseases. We can imagine that as Jesus attended to these people individually and listened to their story, undoubtedly, their pain and suffering would have deeply affected him. After responding to the demands of the crowd, perhaps some deeper questions were arising in his heart concerning his personal calling in life, and perhaps he was experiencing the personal cost of extending himself to the crowd.

We do not know exactly what went on in Jesus' heart but what he does "at daybreak" the next morning communicates that Jesus was a man who marked personal boundaries and knew when to say, "Enough!" Like any of us, Jesus had personal needs that he gave priority to and at times he put his needs over the needs of other people without feeling any guilt.

Saying "No"

In this Scripture, Jesus doesn't get up and, like a machine, carry on responding to the demands of the crowd risking personal "burn out". Instead, aware of his limits, Jesus departs the house and goes to a deserted place, creating a personal boundary. Jesus' primary need was soul care which meant separating himself from people and finding a space to be alone with God. In these spaces, Jesus was re-energised as were his passion, purpose and meaning. By practising this boundary, Jesus was able to do his ministry work free from burn out but even more so, it kept him full of God - full of grace, truth and life – empowering him to compassionately and generously respond to the needs of people and the interruptions and crises situations that naturally unfolded during his ministry.

When we are too deeply affected and stirred up by demanding events or encounters in our life or when something we attend to comes with a big personal cost either physically, emotionally, mentally, spiritually, or psychologically, Jesus invites us to practise boundaries and to find a space to nurture soul care. Believing that we are worthy of loving ourselves is key to doing it.

It is not a matter of overextending ourselves, getting more and more fatigued and then, finally taking a break. Rather, it is about being proactive while going through stressful events and practising our boundaries regularly by creating a space for self-nurturing. This will benefit the wellness of our whole being.

Apart from the boundary of creating space for personal soul care, in this Scripture, Jesus practices a second fundamental boundary – saying "no!" Once the crowds reach Jesus, they "try to prevent him from leaving them". We can imagine that the crowd gave Jesus all sorts of reasons why he should stay with them: some still needed to be cured; others felt loved and cared for by him, others wanted to hear more of his message, others wanted to bring their friends to meet him, others wanted to get to know him more. Similarly, when we are saying "no" or pulling out of something, be it helping someone, leaving a job, walking away from a relationship, declining an invitation, declining a new role at work people may suggest to us reasons why we should change our minds.

I imagine that this crowd was putting a lot of pressure on Jesus to stay with them but he didn't submit to it. Again, Jesus practises boundaries and says a very clear "no!" and responds, "I must proclaim the good news of the kingdom of God to the other cities also; for I was sent for this purpose." Jesus knows that boundaries are necessary to achieve his purpose and inevitably, this will mean not pleasing the crowd, nor winning their approval. He acts with integrity and is true to his deepest self by saying "no!" without feeling any guilt.

As we delve into the gospels we see that there were many people to whom Jesus said "no!" and didn't help and if Jesus did help someone, he expected them to do their part, for example: the woman he saved from being stoned who he asked not to sin anymore[63], the blind man who needed to walk far to wash mud out of his eyes at the pool of Siloam[64], the paralysed man who needed to get up and pick up his mat and walk[65].

We may also find it encouraging seeing how Jesus said "no!" to inappropriate behaviour: he says no to abuse, for example, he slips through the crowd who want to throw him over the cliff[66], he says no to entitlement, for example, he doesn't give in to his mother and brothers who tried to use their relationship with him to pull him away from the crowd he was ministering to[67], he says no to baiting questions, for example, he answers the religious leaders baiting questions with incisive questions of his own[68], he says no to cynicism, for example, he said no to Herod's mocking demand, "Show us a sign that you are the Son of God"[69], he says no to pride, for example, he didn't heal those who were too proud to trust him[70].

By looking at how Jesus practised boundaries, we can learn that it is healthy to say "no!" to people and to live within our personal limitations. Practising boundaries is the secret to feeling well within our own skin because saying "no!" means living with integrity and being true to ourselves. Like Jesus, this will mean speaking the truth in love.

---

63 John 8:1-11 "...Then Jesus stood up again and said to the woman, "Where are your accusers? Didn't even one of them condemn you?" "No, Lord," she said. And Jesus said, "Neither do I. Go and sin no more."
64 John 9:7 ""Go," he told him, "wash in the Pool of Siloam" (this word means "Sent"). So the man went and washed."
65 John 5:8 "Then Jesus said to him, "Get up! Pick up your mat and walk", and he came home seeing.
66 Luke 4:28-30
67 Matthew 12:46-50
68 Matthew 21:23-27, 22:15-22
69 Luke 23:8-9
70 Matthew 13:58

Experiencing the Scripture through prayer, visualisation and art
(Suggested materials: an A4 or A3 drawing book, crayons, paints or coloured pencils)

1. On a fresh page you may like to put the title: "Saying No!".
2. Read the Scripture verse of Luke 4:42-44 slowly and try to absorb the words.
3. Try to visualise what this scene looks like. As you visualise it, what do you find most striking about Jesus (his ability to practise boundaries: that is, creating some personal space for himself, not being manipulated by the crowd…)?
4. Can you name situations in your life where you find it difficult to practise boundaries? Try to visualise yourself creating a boundary or saying "no" if that is what is necessary in your situation(s)?
5. Spend time drawing what practising boundaries, looks like for you? You may want to put some words to your drawing like "No!", "Don't please", "Walk away", "Time off"…
6. As you visualise yourself putting boundaries try to name what you are feeling (empowered, strengthened, encouraged…)?
7. Whenever you feel you are struggling to practise healthy boundaries, you may like to come back to this drawing and allow yourself to be encouraged by what your reflection.

The Scripture experienced in my life

A few days after praying this reading, one evening, there was a power outage in my block of units. During the course of it, there was a knock at my door and the voice of a young male on the other side announcing that he was my new neighbour. Because there was total darkness, I could not see anything through my peep hole. I asked him what he wanted and he replied, "Can I come in because I don't have any candles or a torch". I felt his request was inappropriate, first, because I had never met him and secondly, because we were in darkness. I told him "No! I can't let you in".

Afterwards, I shared about this event with others and had all sorts of reactions! Some thought that I was being cruel and said that they would have let the man in. However, even after listening to what they would have done, I didn't feel guilty for saying "no!" because in the moment I felt very vulnerable and was afraid that by letting the stranger in I was putting my safety at risk. By practising boundaries and saying "no!" to this person, I felt that I was being true to myself as I listened to the wisdom of my body in this situation.

Your experience of Scripture through prayer, visualisation and art

You may like to take some time to journal about how you have experienced this Scripture reading through art and what it has conveyed to you about your own personal journey. This may be helpful to refer back to in the future.

Honouring Needs

HONOURING NEEDS CANNOT BE CONFUSED with being selfish. A need is something necessary or required. When we talk about honouring needs, we are talking about honouring what is necessary or required for us to be healthy and well and these needs may be big or small. For example, one person may need to live in a space that is uncluttered because this aids mental space and for another, their need may be an additional ten minute break at work to make an important phone call for a matter that is absorbing them while they are working.

There is a difference between needs and wants. We can want something but it may not be a necessity for our well-being. Selfishness is usually connected with getting and doing what we want when we want and without caring about the impact it will have on others. For example, I may want to blast my music at midnight and if I do it will surely upset all my neighbours, or I may not be able to find a parking spot so I take the spot marked "Disabled", inconveniencing someone who is disabled.

All of us have needs, although our needs will vary depending on our age, health, and our personal circumstances. Sometimes our needs are met; and, at other times, they remain unmet.

One of the reasons why our needs are unmet is because we fail to voice them. Sadly, this is often the case for survivors of sexual abuse who have struggled to have a voice. Another reason is that in the past our needs have been dishonoured. For those who were sexually abused as children, our needs were violently violated by our perpetrators, particularly the need for our body to be respected, as well as our need for safety and protection. When our needs have been dishonoured from such a young age, the danger is that we may go through the rest of our life accustomed to not having our needs met or minimizing and dismissing them. Ultimately, we may end up feeling very frustrated, angry, depressed and bitter.

Learning to honour our physical, mental, emotional, psychological or spiritual needs will help move us forward on our healing journey.

Honouring our needs is connected to a healthy self-love and self-care. When we honour our needs, we are saying, "I love and care for myself enough to attend to my need. I am worthy. I am important." For survivors of sexual abuse, this may be challenging. At times, honouring our needs may require us to stop in the middle of our busy routines or it may require us to leave our routines for a longer period. Sometimes, honouring our needs may mean sacrificing other things, such as our job, a place that has had significance for us, or friends; and this will be difficult for us.

Even though attempting to honour our needs may mean forfeiting other things, it will benefit our deeper well-being.

In the Scriptures, we can see that Jesus was a person who not only honoured his own needs but also the needs of those who were closest to him. He can teach us what it means to honour our own needs and the needs of others.

The Scripture Reading

The apostles gathered together with Jesus and reported all they had done and taught. He said to them, 'Come away by yourselves to a deserted place and rest a while.' People were coming and going in great numbers and they had no opportunity even to eat. So they went off in the boat by themselves to a deserted place.

Mark 6:30-32

In the biblical context, this Scripture reading comes directly after we hear about the death of Jesus' cousin, John the Baptist who was beheaded under the order of King Herod.[71] After learning about this, his disciples go and get the body of John and lay him in a tomb.

We can, therefore, imagine that in these verses when the disciples gathered around Jesus, the first report they gave him was the sad and disturbing news of his cousin's death. Undoubtedly, this would have grieved Jesus profoundly.

---

71 Mark 6:17-29

Impressively, even in his grief-stricken state, Jesus remains sensitive to the needs of his disciples, noticing that they are tired and haven't had time to eat because of their busyness with the crowds.

Jesus doesn't dismiss or minimise his disciples' needs and expect them to push beyond their limits like a machine. Instead, he honours their needs with a practical invitation to "Come away to a deserted place to rest a while". What a beautiful display of Jesus' humanity and compassion! Through this gesture, Jesus was teaching his disciples about the importance of honouring their needs and showing them that it was okay to break their routine and change their plans to meet their needs. At the same time, Jesus was also honouring his own need for time and space to process the tragic death of his cousin and what this was implying for his own public ministry.

Jesus teaches us that it is important to honour our needs whether they are physical, emotional, psychological or spiritual.

Experiencing the Scripture through prayer, visualisation and art
(Suggested materials: an A4 or A3 drawing book, crayons, paints or coloured pencils)

1. On a fresh page you may like to put the title: "Honouring Needs".
2. Read the Scripture verse of Mark 6:30-32 slowly and try to visualise the scene. If you can, visualise yourself in the scene as one of the disciples who is gathered around Jesus.
3. You may like to draw the scene as you have visualised it.
4. Reflect on your current needs: physical, emotional, psychological and spiritual. You may like to write your needs on your picture.
5. Try to visualise Jesus gazing lovingly at you and acknowledging your needs.
6. Jesus' way of honouring his disciples' needs was by inviting them to, "Come away… to a deserted place and rest for a while". As Jesus gazes at you with love, do you have an intuition of how he may be inviting you to honour your needs?

What would it require of you to honour your needs?
(You may like to write on your picture what you understand.)
7. If you have named several needs, prioritise them from most to least important.
8. As you look at what you have visualised, how does it make you feel?
9. How does the thought of honouring your needs change the perception you have of yourself (for example: makes you feel "I am important" as opposed to "I'm not important", or "My needs matter" as opposed to "My needs don't matter", or "I am worthy enough" as opposed to "I don't deserve to have my needs met")?

The Scripture experienced in my life

Recently, I had some major surgery. Although the surgery went well, the post-op period was very challenging due to complications I didn't count on. Prior to the surgery, I had organised what I considered would be sufficient sick leave from work for my recovery. On the final days of my leave, it was clear to me that I would need more time to recover physically.

Apart from dealing with the physical consequences of the surgery, I was also attending to a number of issues around the prosecution case and seeking justice. The time, as well as the physical, mental and emotional energy that these required, was constant and I was feeling anxious and overwhelmed at the thought of trying to deal with these major issues while working and, even more so, while recovering from surgery.

I reflected on how I could best honour my needs and the needs of those I minister to. I thought about the fact that I would have only one opportunity to resolve the events around seeking justice through the pending court trial, as well as, intermediations with the Church. I wanted to give it my all so that I could move forward, knowing that I have done everything possible to deal with the matter. I didn't want to look back down the track having regrets or thinking "What if I had...?" or "I wonder if...?"

I thought about how stressful I was finding it to deal with these matters while working and how they absorbed me during my work, not allowing me to give my best to those I was ministering to. Aware that my attention was divided made me feel that I would not be able to carry out my ministry with integrity. This made me question if I was being just to those I ministered to.

I felt that the best way to honour my needs at the time was to ask for an extended period of leave that would enable me to see all these matters through, giving them my undivided attention. I prayed about it for some days before making an appointment to see my manager.

I knew that there was a huge risk that my manager would tell me it was not possible and that if this is what I needed, they could not hold the position for me. The thought of resigning made me feel very sad, first, because I was passionate about my ministry and secondly, because my colleagues were inspirational, supportive and nurturing.

After some days of prayer, I chose to take the risk and ask my manager for what I needed. I was as open as I could be about my needs and the response I received was very compassionate. My manager assured me that she did not see a problem with my request and that my job would still be there for me to return to. Above that, she assured me if I came to the end of my leave and feeling that I still needed more time to resolve these issues, more leave could be arranged.

I can't forget the huge weight that I immediately felt lifted off my shoulders when my manager responded compassionately to my need and it greatly benefited me to be able to attend to these pending matters, giving them my undivided attention. Needless to mention, my anxiety and stress levels have been greatly reduced.

Your experience of Scripture through prayer, visualisation and art

You may like to take some time to journal about how you have experienced this Scripture reading through art and what it has conveyed to you about your own personal journey. This may be helpful to refer back to in the future.

Fracturing Shame

SHAME AND GUILT CAN BE taken to mean the same but they are distinct. Shame is personal and concerns oneself, while guilt is public and concerns others. Shame makes us feel, "I am bad" while guilt makes us feel, "I did something bad". Shame reflects on the "human being" and guilt reflects on the "human doing". Shame makes me feel I have failed to meet my own standards of behaviour. Guilt makes me feel I have failed to meet others' standards of behaviour. The voice of shame says to us, "you have not done your best" while guilt says to us, "you have harmed another". Shame leads to internal validations, "I feel bad" while guilt leads to external validations, "I will be punished".[72]

Shame can be detected through our physiological responses. We may go "red" or "flushed" in the face, or we may want to withdraw or hide, or we will hang our head down or look away.

Survivors of sexual abuse are well acquainted with both guilt and shame. Guilt can be one of the biggest challenges for survivors. We feel like, "I did something bad!" Perhaps guilt is our mind's way of protecting us as we suddenly experience that our life has been turned upside down; our world is no longer safe, it is no longer predictable, and nothing makes sense. Somehow guilt gives us a sense of being in control again. Blaming ourselves for what we did or didn't do and saying, "It was my fault!" may provide a sense of safety and feeling we are in control.

Blaming ourselves may also be encouraged by others. Often, when survivors reveal to family or friends that they have been sexually abused, instead of finding support, comments are made suggesting we are to blame: "But they're such a nice/good person", "they would never do anything like that"… People don't want it to be true! Just as we feel unsafe after being sexually abused, so may those with whom we share our experience; and consequently, they may cast their own fears onto us saying: "they (the accused) wouldn't do that", "you're a

---

[72] Listening to Shame, Brene Brown, March 2012, TED Talk, http://www.ted.com/talks/brene_brown_listening_to_shame

liar", "it was your fault", "you imagined it". These messages are reinforced with more strength when they come from other people. Eventually, the guilt builds up into an overwhelming shame and we go from feeling like, "I did something bad" to believing, "I am a bad person".

Our belief of our worthiness to be loved and to love is connected to shame. Shame leads us to believe that we are not worthy of love or deserve to have a good life because of our imperfections or what has happened to us. This belief is crippling and prevents us from looking forward to a future of new possibilities.

The truth is that our guilt and shame can be dissolved and healed. Through the Scripture story below, Jesus invites us to experience the power he has to set us free from our guilt and shame.

The Scripture Reading

Now he was teaching in one of the synagogues on the Sabbath. And just then there appeared a woman with a spirit that had crippled her for eighteen years. She was bent over and was quite unable to stand up straight. When Jesus saw her, he called her over and said, "Woman, you are set free from your ailment." When he laid his hands on her, immediately she stood up straight and began praising God.

Luke 13:10-13

This Scripture tells of a woman whose back is so "bent over" that she's "unable to stand up straight". Can we imagine what that's like? All this woman sees is the ground and whatever is at its level: dirt, rubbish, grass, flowers, weeds, and people's feet rushing around her. The woman couldn't look forward or upward to see the possibilities before her. Due to her illness (that could have been arthritis), this woman never viewed the world around her in its full perspective; she could never view a person's full stature and speak to them face to face, she could never see a house in full view, she could never look up to appreciate the beauty of the tall green trees or see the blue or moonlit sky. Her whole perspective of life was also crippled!

It's inevitable that this illness also caused her to suffer mentally, emotionally, spiritually and psychologically. I imagine the frustration and anger she must have felt not to be able to do the things that we do so easily, like sitting at a table, eating and swallowing food, choosing food at the market, crossing a busy street, hanging clothes up on line, opening up a window, dressing herself. I imagine the despair and depression she would have experienced for the fact that her quality of life had been greatly reduced and limited for eighteen years. I imagine how terribly alone and isolated she must have felt, particularly in the religious context where the belief was that illness was a punishment from God for one's sins. Hence, she would have been pronounced "Unclean!" and forced to live on the margins of her faith community. People would have avoided contact with her and stayed at a distance to her.

Imagine the spiritual impacts of this! The people's harsh judgment would have led her to ask God, "Why me? Why this illness? What did I do to deserve it? It's not fair!" Undoubtedly, she would have been sensitive to people looking down on her and heard them murmuring, "She must have committed some big sins to be that crippled!"

Imagine how this would have affected the women's self-image! Indeed, she would have been plagued with guilt and shame. Originally, she may have been wracked with guilt and blamed herself saying, "I must have done something bad to deserve this". Gradually, over an eighteen year period, and largely aided by people's judgment of her, the guilt may have shifted to overwhelming shame and led her to believe, "I am bad" and "I am unworthy of love or deserving of a good life".

Shame and guilt bends us down so that our perception of ourselves is twisted and skewed. Our vision is cast downwards and we end up only ever seeing the dirt in our life and the bad side of things that happen to us. This bent over woman symbolises any person who is stunted and plagued by guilt and shame. Often, this is the case of survivors of sexual abuse.

I'm certain that the woman did not anticipate how her life was about to change when she entered the synagogue! Jesus notices her when she walks in and he calls her to come to him. Imagine the embarrassment she felt being singled out and having all eyes drawn to her. To get to where Jesus was in the synagogue would have meant that she needed to pass through the mens area which would have been scandalous (men and women were segregated in the synagogue. The men gathered at the front and women stayed in the side area, sitting on benches in rows against the wall). The next thing Jesus does is even more scandalous. He lays his hands on her and tells her that she is free from whatever it is that is twisting her body and deforming her. This is a woman who had previously been deemed "unclean"!

The next scandal is the fact that it is the Sabbath when Jesus heals this woman (it was forbidden to heal on the Sabbath). It may have crossed Jesus' mind to wait until sundown to heal her but he may have thought in his mind that this woman has already waited long enough for healing (eighteen years) and now was the time to respond to the desperate needs of her body and soul. Love, compassion, mercy and kindness go beyond any law for Jesus.

For the first time in eighteen years, the woman is able to straighten up and look forward and upward and the first thing she would have seen was the face of Jesus. How beautiful!

Her whole being was healed: body, mind and spirit. People would no longer question what sin she committed in her past. Jesus' healing touch completely dissolved the woman's guilt and shame restoring her to a healthy perception of self. From now the woman could believe she is worthy of love and a good life. It's awesome how dramatic the change was for this woman after a single encounter with Jesus. Surely, the woman experienced her healing as the greatest gift she would receive in her life-time. She responds immediately, praising God.

Today Jesus offers us the same gift. He "sees" what weighs us down and bends us over. While it may not be a crippling physical disease, it may be something bending us down spiritually, mentally, emotionally or psychologically and distorting everything we see. Jesus is not indifferent to our pain and suffering and he feels deep compassion for us.

Whether our burden is the guilt or shame that we have held for many years, or something different, through the Scripture, Jesus invites us to "Come to him".

Our life can change radically as it did for the woman in this story. If we come forward to Jesus, he is not afraid to get close enough to touch and heal us. He is ready to fracture the guilt and shame that we have held on to for so many years and to gently bend us back into shape so that we can also begin to look upward and forward to new possibilities in our life.

Jesus wants us to know that we are worthy of love and deserving of a good life by saying to us the same words he said to the woman, "X (put your name there), you are set free from your ailment (name whatever it may be for you, i.e. shame, guilt…)", "Be set free from the shame of sexual abuse and stand straight! Be set free from the burden of blame that people put on you and stand straight! I don't judge you. I don't blame you. I don't condemn you. I feel compassion for you and want you to have life. You are worthy of love. I love you. Be healed. Look upward and forward and see life with a new perspective. Let me fracture your shame once and for all."

If we want, Jesus has the power to heal our shame from sexual abuse that has bound us for so long. We don't need to keep living our life "bent down". It is time to "stand up straight" and to look forward! Let's allow Jesus' love to encourage us to do this.

Experiencing the Scripture through prayer, visualisation and art
(Suggested materials: an A4 or A3 drawing book, crayons, paints or coloured pencils)

1. On a fresh page, you may like to put the title: "Fracturing Shame".
2. Read the Scripture verse of Luke 13:10-13 slowly and try to visualise the scene. If you can, visualise yourself in the place of this woman who enters in the synagogue while Jesus is teaching.
3. Reflect on what it is in your life that makes you "bent down" and "unable to stand up straight".
4. Try to visualise yourself among the women in the synagogue and then you hear Jesus saying to you, "Come here!" What do you feel as you visualise the scene?
   What do you feel as you visualise yourself coming forward to the front where Jesus stands?

5. Visualise Jesus laying his hands on you and saying to you, "X (put your name here), you are set free of your ailment (give it a name)".
6. Visualise how a life free of your "ailment" looks?
You may want to spend time drawing what you have visualised.
7. As you look at your drawing, what does it communicate to you? You may want to sum it up in a couple of words that you can write in your drawing (for example: hope, freedom, restoration).

When you are struggling with shame in the future, you may like to come back to this Scripture reading and drawing as a reminder of your reflection on "fracturing shame".

The Scripture experienced in my life

I was invited to do a pre-recorded radio interview about my last book[73] and I accepted the invitation.

I was quite nervous leading up to the invitation and more so, on the day of the interview. The person interviewing me had a lovely calming personality which put me at ease before we initiated the interview.

About half-way through the interview, as I was describing the spiritual impacts of sexual abuse and talking about how we often feel like, "I am the one who did something bad" and "I am bad", the shame of the abuse began arising in me again (probably not evident to the listeners). I am aware that the same feelings I experienced at the time of the sexual abuse can emerge again when I speak of the event. This was happening as I was being interviewed. As I articulated the personal emotional impacts of my trauma, my body was remembering what it felt like at the time.

By the end of the interview I felt an overwhelming sense of shame. I said to the radio presenter, "I feel like it went badly. I couldn't articulate what I wanted to say!" What I was failing to realise is that the shame of the abuse had resurfaced in me making me feel that "I am bad!" and "It went badly". The radio

---

73 *Child, Arise! The Courage to Stand. A Spiritual Handbook for Survivors of Sexual Abuse*

presenter assured me that it went very well. I felt like crawling under the table of the studio and hiding.

I made my way home and I was contemplating the thought of getting under the covers of my bed and taking a break from the world. I attempted to let the adult me speak to my inner child (the one who was re-living the shame) and we agreed that instead of crawling into bed it would be better to deal with the shame.

I picked up this story from Scripture and visualised myself as the "bent down" woman. It wasn't hard! My shame was bending me so far down that I was back there in the dirt of the sexual abuse. In that moment, my self-perception and perception of the world was crippled by my shame.

As I read the Scripture slowly, I pictured Jesus seeing me feeling full of shame and inviting me to come closer to him. I felt "I am not worthy" or "good enough" to be close to Jesus (God) but I visualised myself coming forward towards Jesus with my head hanging low. When I was close to Jesus, he extended his hands ever so gently on my head and he said to me, "Jane, be set free from the shame of sexual abuse! Be set free from the control that your shame has over you that prevents you from standing tall! Be set free from the lies that your shame tells you – that you are unworthy of love and don't deserve to have a good life! Be set free from what shame makes you believe about yourself - you are bad – because the truth is that you are - very good – I know because I created you![74]" Jesus repeated these words like a mantra and as he did I began to experience my shame shifting within me and a lightness of heart evolving.

I felt my thoughts were also shifting from how badly I felt about the interview to realising what I had achieved by doing it – I had now made my voice public – and I spoke the truth publicly, both were "very good" things. I realised how my shame distorted my perception of the radio interview.

As I felt Jesus' gentle hands on my head, I felt within myself that my shame was being "straightened out" so that I began to feel some "good" pride. When I lifted my head, I was looking straight at Jesus' face. I saw a profound love in his eyes as he looked at me. He made me feel that I am worthy of being loved

---

[74] Genesis 1:31

and deserve to have a good life. He taught me that shame is not permanently ingrained in our DNA, it can be healed and he can heal it.

What a great gift I received! I can now look forward to a future of having a voice and I look upwards with a grateful heart to Jesus for this opportunity to fracture my shame.

Your experience of Scripture through prayer, visualisation and art

You may like to take some time to journal about how you have experienced this Scripture reading through art and what it has conveyed to you about your own personal journey. This may be helpful to refer back to in the future.

Releasing Pain

NO ONE LIKES PAIN. WHEN we feel emotional pain, we want it to go away. Instinctively, we run from it, push it away, or make ourselves numb so we can't feel it. Running away from pain is only a temporary solution that may lead to bigger problems like physical illness, increased stress, anxiety, or emotional numbness.

For survivors of sexual abuse, experiencing pain as an adult can reopen childhood wounds. Therefore dealing with pain is challenging. When traumatic memories of the past are triggered by experiences of pain, we may find ourselves reverting back to behaviours that belonged to the traumatic event; behaviours that don't seem to be logical in the present situation.

While it may briefly feel "good" to run away from pain, our body continues to harbour it. If we can learn to feel our pain as we feel joy or frustration, we will live a fulfilled life. When we don't allow ourselves to feel pain, we also deny ourselves the pleasure of feeling positive emotions. It is difficult to believe but learning to face our pain, and releasing it in our lives will lead us to freedom and happiness; key to this, however, is releasing it in ways that are healthy and constructive leading to restoration of our person. Sadly, people may release their pain in ways that are destructive and harmful to their person.

It can be difficult for survivors of sexual abuse to release strong negative emotions. For those who experienced sexual abuse as children, we were sworn to secrecy by our perpetrator which meant holding on to all the negative emotions that we experienced. As children, our perpetrator denied us the possibility of releasing pain. As adults, learning to release our pain is also about undoing the unhealthy "holding on" to emotions that we learned and giving ourselves permission to release painful emotions. I would suggest the benefits of seeking professional help to learn to do this and in the case of any physical symptoms you may experience, consulting with a doctor.

If it is any consolation at all, Jesus, even though he was God's Son, suffered pain as part of his human condition. Some of the gospel stories, particularly the

Passion accounts, reveal Jesus releasing pain in his life. He teaches us that not only is pain natural to our human condition, but so is the need to release it!

The Scripture Reading

When Mary came to where Jesus was and saw him, she knelt at his feet and said to him, "Lord, if you had been here, my brother would not have died." When Jesus saw her weeping, and the Jews who came with her also weeping, he was greatly disturbed in spirit and deeply moved. He said, "Where have you laid him?" They said to him, "Lord, come and see." Jesus began to weep.

John 11:32-35

"Then Jesus, crying with a loud voice, said, "Father, into your hands I commend my spirit." Having said this, he breathed his last."

Luke 23:46

"At three o'clock, Jesus cried out in a loud voice, "Eloi, Eloi, lema sabachthani?" which means "My God, my God, why have you forsaken me?"

Mark 15:34

In each of these Scripture verses Jesus is suffering pain; in the latter two Scriptures, it is excruciating pain, so excruciating that Jesus needs to release it.

The first Scripture verses from the Gospel of John are an excerpt from the story of the death of Lazarus. Lazarus and his sisters, Martha and Mary, were friends of Jesus. We know from the gospels that Jesus would visit and dine with them.[75] In these particular verses, Jesus has heard about Lazarus' death and is coming to see Martha and Mary. Mary releases her pain with Jesus as she kneels at his feet weeping, "Lord, if you had been here, my brother would not have died!" Mary's pain is heart-felt.

Jesus responds with great empathy as he becomes "greatly disturbed in spirit and moved".

---

75   Luke 10:38-42; John 11:1; John 12:1-3

The first step to face our pain is to feel it. To feel our pain, we need to allow it to arise in our body and notice the sensations that occur with it, without manipulating or controlling it by trying to push it down or numb it. Feeling our pain means being present to it and acknowledging that it is there. If it is helpful, talk to your pain as you would connect to your inner child… "I can hear your pain and feel it! I am listening to your pain! I am here with you in your pain".

When we acknowledge our pain, the first thing we may notice is that we become "disturbed" and "moved" in our spirit just like Jesus in this Scripture story. Secondly, we may experience this translating into our physical body as we begin to get restless, agitated, irritated, distressed… we may notice a change in our breathing, our body may begin to tremor, we may break out into a sweat… the emotional pain begins to show in our physical body. We may find ourselves asking, what next? What do I do with pain?

Jesus teaches us healthy forms of releasing pain from our bodies. Once the pain moves Jesus in his spirit, he moves physically. Moving our body is a very healthy form of releasing pain. Jesus releases his pain meaningfully through a gesture of love towards Mary involving physical movement. He wants to go and see where Lazarus has been buried!

Moving our body when we feel pain is an effort but if we don't, we may find ourselves falling into an even deeper downward spiral. Going outside for a walk or a run, doing some gentle exercise, going for a swim, doing some gardening or something that involves movement will help to get the energy flowing and release pain that is stuck. By moving our body, we are saying to our pain "I know you are there and I will attend to you!" It is how we can show love to ourselves.

For you, a meaningful way of releasing your pain could be by showing gestures of love towards others and this may require moving your body. For example, offering to do an elderly neighbour's shopping would mean a trip to the shops, baking a cake for your colleagues would mean being active in the kitchen, or inviting a friend to come over for dinner similarly means a trip to the shop for the ingredients and coming home to prepare the meal. Releasing pain in meaningful ways involves creativity but, in the process, we experience the pain shifting and being transformed into love. There are many examples in the gospels where we see Jesus creatively releasing his pain through gestures of love: he miraculously feeds a crowd of five thousand people just after he has heard the sad news about the death of his cousin, John the Baptist,[76] the night before Jesus dies, he washes the feet of his disciples[77] and eats a meal with them,[78] following his last supper, he walks with his disciples to the Garden of Gethsemane where he prayerfully releases his pain and anguish to God.[79]

In the story of Lazarus' death, when the people invite Jesus to "come and see" where Lazarus is buried, Jesus began to weep. Crying and weeping is another way of releasing pain from our bodies. Sometimes we find it hard to believe that even though Jesus was God's Son, he wept! But here we have it – Jesus wept. God shows us through Jesus who is human just like us, that it is healthy to release pain through tears and crying.

We may find that once we allow our pain to be released through tears that we cry…a lot. This is not unusual for survivors of childhood sexual abuse. When we were children, we weren't permitted to release our pain through tears so don't be surprised if once we give ourselves permission to release our pain that we find we cry tears that have been stored up since childhood. It may be helpful to find some good support from a close friend or health professional as we release pain in our lives. If we don't have support around us, it is consoling to know that in the same way that Jesus supported Mary as she wept, he is present and supporting us as we weep.

In the last two Scriptures that are in the context of Jesus' crucifixion and death, reference is made to Jesus "crying out in a loud voice". The meaning of this description closer to the Greek translation is - Jesus "screamed" - which would have been very appropriate for the excruciating pain that Jesus was suffering. In these Scriptures, Jesus doesn't scream out into the empty space, he screams out to God in prayer. I emphasise "to" God and not "at" God. There is a difference between screaming "at" someone and screaming out "to" someone. To scream "at" someone is directing what we are feeling toward that person while screaming out "to" someone is getting them involved in what we are feeling.

---

76   Mark 6:27-44
77   John 13:3-5
78   Luke 22:14-15
79   Matthew 26:36-46

As Jesus screams out to God his father, "My God, my God, why have you forsaken me?" and his last words, "Father, into your hands I commend my spirit", he prayerfully releases his pain. I have heard people saying that screaming is not God-like! But here we have it, God screams out in the person of Jesus. Although Jesus was fully divine, what we often forget is that he was also fully human, experiencing the same human limitations that we do. Saying this, care needs to be taken not to misinterpret it. It doesn't give us permission to go around "screaming" at people in a way that is undignifying and destructive to the person at the receiving end. If we release pain through screaming, Jesus invites us to do it constructively.

Using our voice to release pain is very cathartic. Screaming out helps propel the energy of pain out of our bodies and leaves us feeling more peaceful. One way of prayerfully releasing pain is to go to a place out in the open when there are few people around (for example, a big park, standing on the beach before the sea…) and scream out to God… Let your pain out through your voice… scream out to God whatever is at the bottom of your heart without trying to control or manipulate it. You may just scream out, "Why, God? Why?", "What did I do to deserve this?", "Where are you, God?"

If you can't find a place out in the open, another way of releasing pain is by getting a pillow, putting your face into it and screaming out as hard as you can until you feel you can't anymore! You may want to scream out to God or you may find you don't have words, and if that's the case, you may just want to scream out with loud continuous groans of "Aaarrrgggghhhh!"

The above may work for some people but not for others. You may have other ways of releasing your pain. Different things work for different people. Some people find journaling useful, others draw or paint, others release pain by playing a musical instrument, others like manually building something, others release it through dancing. The most important thing is to find what works best for you.

When we release pain in our body, we can feel it. It is like something breaks open from within us and we feel it going through us and leaving our body. We feel an energy release and consequently we may feel lighter and even have a sense of freedom as something heavy and pressing is no longer with us or is felt much less than prior to the release.

So let's be encouraged by a very human Jesus who needed to release his pain. As we learn to release our pain, may we experience the freedom that comes from doing it.

Experiencing the Scripture through prayer, visualisation and art
(Suggested materials: an A4 or A3 drawing book, crayons, paints or coloured pencils)

1. On a fresh page, you may like to put the title: "Releasing Pain".
2. Read the Scripture verses slowly and try to visualise the scenes. It may be helpful for you to visualise yourself as either Mary or one of the mourners in the crowd who followed her and you may be one of the bystanders at Jesus' cross.
3. As you are visualising the scene, what calls your attention? It may be a "crying" or "screaming" Jesus.
4. What is being stirred in you as you visualise the scene? Do not be surprised if you experience some pain arising in you. If this happens, allow it to arise and feel it.
5. What is your pain about (you may find it helpful to spend some time journaling)?
6. Take time to visualise your pain being released from your body? What image comes to mind?
7. You may find it helpful trying to draw on your page what you have visualised. What does releasing pain look like to you?
   (If there is something you find more helpful, take advantage of this chapter to practise it.)
8. As you look at your drawing, what does it say to you about releasing pain? How would you sum it up in three words?

9. Has there been some shift in you today (in your emotional state, in your beliefs about pain…)?

Next time you experience pain arising within yourself, you may find it helpful to come back to this chapter and drawing and allow it to remind you about the benefits of releasing pain.

The Scripture experienced in my life

Recently, I needed to have some major surgery. The surgery went well but I had many post-surgery challenges which meant that I was in hospital longer than anticipated.

Only a few days after being discharged from hospital, I began to experience unbearable pain. Immediately, I went back to the Emergency Department and after waiting a very long four hours in pain I was attended to.

Initially, the doctors did some physical examinations during which I was screaming with pain. I would not refer to myself as a "screaming" person. Even when I experience pain, be it physical or emotional, I am normally discreet about it and I don't like to show that I am in pain. I know that this resilience to pain has come from my traumatic past and the fact that I was not permitted to show pain or express it. On this occasion, however, it was different.

As the night went on, my pain became worse. On two occasions, I collapsed in the bathroom as I was screaming out with excruciating pain. The nurses came running in with oxygen and attended to me. It felt like the pain was absorbing every ounce of energy that I had in my body and it left me completely drained and exhausted. I remember thinking, "How am I going to get through this?" I felt done and dusted so to speak!

Finally, the doctors were able to work out what was causing my pain through another physical examination which was very intrusive. As the doctors were proceeding with it, I screamed out so loud that I am sure my screams resonated throughout the whole Emergency Department. I never imagined that I would be able to scream so loud and so hard. I was quite stunned and surprised with myself. As the day went on, I was able to receive effective treatment and, gradually, the pain began to subside.

At the time, I was too preoccupied by what was happening to be reflective about the inner healing that was taking place. A few days later I was able to realise how healing it was to release my pain through screaming. It felt like my screams were coming from a very profound place and not only was I releasing my physical pain but I was also releasing my emotional pain – years of it – experienced from childhood trauma – pain that I was forced to hold on to silently! I do believe that on that day, I released so much pain from my past that was trying desperately to find its way out!

What I am left with, however, is the experience of the freedom that came from releasing my pain through screams and groans! It is true – releasing pain through our voice is very cathartic.

Your experience of Scripture through prayer, visualisation and art

You may like to take some time to journal about how you have experienced this Scripture reading through art and what it has conveyed to you about your own personal journey. This may be helpful to refer back to in the future.

Unwanted Sexual Arousal[80]

ONE OF THE MOST UNCOMFORTABLE impacts that survivors often suffer in silence and struggle to deal with is the persistence of unwanted sexual arousal. Unfortunately, it is inevitable that if a survivor of sexual abuse was sexually aroused during the trauma then the survivor is likely to experience unwanted sexual arousal. In the same way that our body remembers emotions from the time of the trauma, it also remembers physical sensations including sexual arousal. When our trauma is recalled, not only do we re-live the emotions, but we re-experience the physical sensations including sexual arousal. Since the experience of unwanted sexual arousal deepens feelings of shame in survivors, the topic may never arise in counselling or psychological sessions.

Although "unwanted" sexual arousal is an issue that is suffered silently, it does have significant impacts. Some survivors have shared with me the great affliction they experience from unwanted sexual arousal. Dealing with unwanted sexual arousal is emotionally very painful because it reminds survivors of events that we prefer not to remember.

I use the word "unwanted" sexual arousal because that is what it is for survivors —"unwanted"! We don't want to be sexually aroused in a particular moment but it happens and we can't control it! We may not be thinking about or looking at anything sexually stimulating at a particular moment but we become sexually aroused.

Usually, the "unwanted" sexual arousal is brought on when our memory of the trauma is being recalled by a certain trigger. While the triggers for each survivor are distinct, they may be innumerable. A trigger could be anything from:

---

[80] Attempting to deal with the impact of unwanted sexual arousal is very distressing for survivors of sexual abuse. Clearly naming this impact may in itself produce undesired physiological responses in survivors who read this chapter. I will leave it up to survivors to discern if they feel ready enough to read and work through this chapter or not. If survivors find it difficult to work through this on their own, you may prefer to work through it with the support of a psychologist, counsellor or trauma specialist.

a person or object who reminds us of the traumatic event, the body language of a person, the tone of a person's voice, a smell, an activity, a geographical place, a food, a certain taste, a season or time of year, a certain calendar date, events like weddings or a funerals, a song, a movie, an item of clothing… There are loads of things that can act as triggers for survivors leaving us feeling very vulnerable. This means that an unwanted sexual arousal may happen at very inappropriate times and in very inappropriate places causing survivors to experience anguish, shame and isolation.

It is also possible for survivors to wake up with unwanted sexual arousal when experiencing night terrors (nightmares) which is quite distressing and unpleasant.

Unwanted sexual arousal can impact greatly on a survivor's self-esteem. Survivors often feel filthy when they experience unwanted sexual arousal, and are tormented by guilt and shame,[81] even though we have not done anything wrong to cause it. On the contrary, we have been wronged by our perpetrator(s). Nevertheless, we may blame ourselves when we experience unwanted sexual arousal, falsely believing that we have done something to cause it.

It's not true! We have not done anything wrong. We're not to blame. Unwanted sexual arousal happens naturally as our body remembers the traumatic event. The guilt and shame that we experience with unwanted sexual arousal rightfully belongs to our perpetrator(s) and it is important to acknowledge that this impact is a consequence of their crime and grave sin.

Even though we do not want our body to remember the sexual arousal from the time of the abuse, unfortunately, we cannot pick and choose what it remembers but it is through our body remembering that we are being healed. If we can accept this, eventually we can learn not to panic and acknowledge that it is my body's natural way of remembering and healing from the trauma. When it happens, my body is saying, "I am reliving now what you experienced when you were being sexually abused!"

Having said this, dealing with unwanted sexual arousal is very distressing. I personally learned to deal with this impact through prayer. Although prayer

---

81   Our body is remembering how we felt at the time of the traumatic event: "dirty", "filthy", "guilt" and "shame" which we re-experience at the actual time of unwanted sexual arousal.

did not stop the "unwanted" sexual arousals from happening (because they are a natural part of my body's memory of the trauma), it provided me with a space to pour out my heart with Jesus and share my affliction with him. In return, I was able to experience Jesus' unconditional love as he healed areas of my life affected by this impact. When I experienced unwanted sexual arousal, the more I prayed, the more I was able to peacefully accept this as part of my healing process.

The next time you find yourself attempting to deal with this issue you may find the following Scripture helpful.

The Scripture Reading

A leper came to him begging him, and kneeling he said to him, "If you choose, you can make me clean." Moved with pity, Jesus stretched out his hand and touched him, and said to him, "I do choose. Be made clean!" Immediately the leprosy left him, and he was made clean.

Mark 1:40-42

In some of the gospels stories, we see Jesus encountering lepers. During the time of Jesus, leprosy was diagnosed by a priest.[82] The disease was a serious skin condition that was considered to be highly infectious. Once leprosy victims were diagnosed, they were regarded under the religious law as "unclean" and exiled from their communities.[83] Not only did they suffer the physical impacts of this disease, but they also needed to endure multiple spiritual, emotional and psychological impacts.

It is not difficult for me to imagine the leper in this story feeling angry and questioning God, "Why?" , "Why this disease?", "What am I being punished for?", "Why this disease where I am banished from the community of believers?", "What did I do to deserve this?" I can imagine the shame and guilt that this leper would have felt as he "knelt" before Jesus; a shame that had been emphasised even more by the religious law that required him to cover the lower part of his face,

---

82 Leviticus 13:1-44
83 Leviticus 13:45-46

wear torn cloths, have hair unkempt, and cry out, "Unclean! Unclean!"[84] I can imagine the leper questioning God's love for him... "God, if you love me, why did you allow this to happen to me?" I have no doubt that being isolated from his former community and congregation would have had huge psychological and emotional impacts. I am sure that once he was diagnosed and declared "unclean" that the loss and grief he experienced was immediate as all the privileges of being a member of his congregation were taken away from him. Without a doubt, the loneliness and isolation would have impacted his confidence and self-esteem.

Although survivors may not identify with this leper who has a visible skin disease, we may identify with the spiritual, emotional and psychological impacts of his disease, particularly when we experience unwanted sexual arousal that causes us to feel "unclean". The leper's feelings of guilt and shame would be very familiar to us and for survivors who are "Catholic", the guilt and shame may have been even more emphasised by the Church's teaching around sexuality. It is understandable why survivors can become deeply distressed and even angry when these teachings are emphasised because they cause us to feel even more shame and guilt over the "unwanted" sexual arousal; something that is a natural physiological consequence of the sexual abuse experienced at the hands of the Church that is teaching moral standards around sexuality. So the experience of the leper in this story is one that will resonate with survivors of sexual abuse.

The leper, however, has not lost hope. He has obviously heard about Jesus' power to heal all kinds of illnesses and he must think to himself, "I believe he can heal me too!" It meant that the leper needed to come before Jesus and ask for what he needed. The man finds Jesus and comes before him "kneeling" humbly. He makes his request to Jesus, "If you choose to, you can make me clean!" He knows he is risking being rejected by Jesus who had the right to do so according to the Jewish religious law that forbade contact with lepers who were deemed "unclean".[85]

But Jesus does not reject the man. On the contrary, Jesus is moved with pity. He is able to feel the anguish and despair of the leper kneeling before him. He is able to put himself in his skin and understand his affliction. Even

---
84   Leviticus 13:45-46
85   Ref: Numbers 5:2

though Jesus knows if he touches the leper he could be in serious trouble with the religious authorities, as well as be deemed "unclean" himself, he chooses to stretch out his hand and touch the leper. As Jesus touches the man, he says to him, "I do choose. Be made clean!"

What a beautiful person Jesus is! He clearly puts the need of the leper to be healed before the imposed religious law and he chooses to love the leper in a very practical way – he heals him and makes him clean! What courage, what love, what integrity we see in Jesus.

What a beautiful role model Jesus is for all religious leaders of our Church if his example is followed! While the Church seeks how to respond to survivors of sexual abuse, the answer is right before it in the life of Jesus, the One it proclaims, who responds to the needs of poor, the broken and those on the margins of society with love and compassion, healing and restoring them to wholeness and well-being. Through his life, Jesus teaches that the most important law to be kept is the law of LOVE – the greatest commandment of all! If there is no LOVE in religious law, there is no God! Sadly, in many cases leading up to the years of the Royal Commission into Institutional Responses to Child Sexual Abuse (2012-2017), survivors have not been shown the face of God in their dealings with the Church.

Through the healing of this leper in the gospel story, Jesus reveals to him the true face of God… a God who cares and doesn't abandon, a God who hears not one who is deaf, a God with a heart of compassion not a heart of stone, a God who loves not punishes, a God who lifts up and esteems not one who puts down, a God who connects and is inclusive not one who disconnects and is exclusive, a God who wants healing and wholeness not brokenness, a God who frees not binds, a God who wants us to live not die!

Jesus' greatest desire is to reveal the true face of God in our life – LOVE. When we experience "unwanted" sexual arousal and feel "unclean" we too can come before Jesus saying to him, "Jesus, if you choose to, you can make me clean! You can cleanse me of the shame and guilt that I have lived with for years because this happened to me! You can cleanse me of feeling that I have been the cause of this and done something wrong and that this is punishment from you! You can cleanse me of feeling dirty when this happens and the feeling of not being worthy enough to be with people! You can cleanse me of all these things that keep me bound up and don't allow me to be free and live! If you choose to Jesus, you CAN make me clean!"

Visualise Jesus standing before you as you pour out your honest feelings to him. Don't be afraid to say things as they are… there is no need to pretty things up for Jesus… Jesus can handle our raw feelings! When you have finished saying everything to him, visualise Jesus before you gently stretching out his hand to yours and saying to you, "I do choose. Be made clean!" How gracious is Jesus! If we listen more deeply in our heart, perhaps Jesus will reveal to us more of God's heart and feelings. As I listened further, I felt Jesus saying, "I do choose to. You have suffered enough! I don't want to see you broken anymore. I am a God of compassion… a God of love. I want you to experience life not death. I want to make you clean. Be made clean! Be made clean of your shame! Be made clean of guilt! Be made clean of your pain! Be made clean of your worthlessness! You ARE clean… you ARE clean of guilt… you ARE clean of shame… you ARE clean of worthlessness, you ARE clean! YOU ARE CLEAN!"

We don't need to be afraid to come forward to Jesus because the only thing Jesus will show us is the true Love of God. If, like the leper, we come forward to Jesus every time we feel "unclean" from an "unwanted" sexual arousal and we allow Jesus to repeatedly say to us, "Be made clean! You ARE clean!" then gradually, we will experience that we no longer feel shame and guilt for something that is a natural consequence of the sexual abuse. Coming to accept that sexual arousal is a "natural" physiological response provoked by traumatic memory, without burrowing ourselves in shame and guilt, will make our healing journey so much lighter and freeing.

I might add that I was struck by Jesus' selection of words, "Be MADE clean!" To "make" something implies time… a process. It made me reflect on my own healing journey and I realised that it is true. Allowing Jesus to cleanse me of shame and guilt has implied a process that has taken place over time. Experiencing Jesus' healing in my life is a gradual process. So if we feel that the change in ourselves is slow… perhaps it is helpful to remember that we are in the "making" process… There is something happening! If we persist, we will see changes and we will experience being MADE clean.

Hopefully, the steps below will be helpful to assist in this process.

Experiencing the Scripture through prayer, visualisation and art
(Suggested materials: an A4 or A3 drawing book, crayons, paints or coloured pencils)

1. On a fresh page, you may like to put the title: "Unwanted Sexual Arousal".
2. Read the Scripture of Mark 1:4-42 slowly and try to visualise the scene. Try to imagine what it may have been like for the leper to be diagnosed with this disease and expelled from his community? What strikes you about the leper? In what way do you feel identified with the leper?
3. Now try to visualise yourself in this scene as the leper, coming forward to Jesus and bringing with you the spiritual, emotional and psychological impacts of unwanted sexual arousal. As you visualise this, can you articulate the spiritual, emotional and psychological impacts? (for example: shame, guilt, isolation, anger, meaninglessness…)
4. You may like to draw on your page what the scene you are visualising looks like?
5. If you can, visualise yourself in this scene kneeling at the feet of Jesus and saying to him, "If you choose, you can make me clean!" If you are able to, articulate with Jesus exactly what it is that you want to be made clean (that is, the spiritual, emotional and psychological impacts, for example: shame, guilt, anger, isolation…)
6. Visualise Jesus extending his hand out to you despite what you are feeling and saying, "I choose to. Be made clean!"
7. How does Jesus' response to you make you feel? What image of God does Jesus reveal to you through his gesture? (for example: God cares, God wants to heal us…) What does Jesus' gesture reveal to you about God's love? (for example: it's compassionate,

unconditional, gentle…) You may like to write some of these words around your picture.
8. As Jesus says to you, "I choose to. Be made clean", what do you visualise happening within you? Can you somehow draw what this looks like on your picture?
9. Take some time now to look at your picture and reflect on it.
    i) What does it communicate to you about God?
    ii) What does it communicate to you about God's love?
    iii) How does your picture foster hope in you to deal with unwanted sexual arousal? (for example: it may communicate that shame and guilt can be diminished or I can be free of the impacts…)
    iv) Is there something in you that has shifted as you were visualising and drawing? Can you try to name exactly what it is? (it may be your image of God, how you feel now about unwanted sexual arousal…) You may like to write this somewhere on your drawing.

The next time you experience an unwanted sexual arousal, if you are not accessible to your drawing, you may like to recall the words of this Scripture. Stop wherever you are and visualise yourself coming forward to Jesus and saying, "If you choose, you can make me clean!" Visualise Jesus stretching out his hand to you and saying, "I choose to. Be made clean!"

When you are able to, you may find it helpful to draw what this looked like once again. You will be amazed how, over time, your drawings will change so that you notice… you ARE being MADE clean!

The Scripture experienced in my life

Leading up to the trial of my perpetrator, I was required to review the Police Statement I had made four years ago. It was something I knew I needed to do but kept putting off because of the painful consequences that would be inevitable from doing it. Certain circumstances were pressing me to do this and not put it off any longer.

My Statement was long and detailed. As I picked it up to read, I took several deep breaths in and out and I began to read it. As I began to get closer to the part outlining the traumatic events I wanted to stop reading and put it down. I took some more deep breaths in and out, after drinking some water tried to continue. As I got to the part describing the sexual abuse my heart began racing and I felt the same panic and fear that I did at the time of the trauma. I began to have flashbacks and with them came the unwanted sexual arousal. I was very aware at the time that this was happening to me and I tried to accept that this was a natural physiological response of my body to the traumatic memories that were being recalled. I tried to continue reading my Statement. Instinctively, one wants to forget something so tragic, needing to recall it feels like one is torturing oneself!

By the time I reached the end, my body was a complete mess; it was as if my body was re-living the trauma all over again. Not only did I feel the shame and guilt from back then but I also felt shame and guilt for being sexually aroused at that very moment as my body remembered the trauma. It made me feel dirty and worthless and I wanted to hide somewhere where I would not be found.

I recalled this Scripture and in that very spot where I was, I closed my eyes and visualised the Scripture scene before me. I then visualised myself in the current state I was in at the time… I too like this leper felt unclean, I too felt guilt and shame, I too had questions for God. I visualised myself coming forward to Jesus in that state and kneeling before Jesus I said, "If you choose, you can make me clean!" I poured out my heart to Jesus. After expressing all that I felt in my heart, I listened to Jesus saying to me through these words from Scripture, "I choose to. Be made clean!"

At the time, it felt like Jesus' outstretched hand absorbed all my shame and guilt. It was as if Jesus had cleaned it all up. Although the physiological response was still there, through visualisation and prayer, I felt light in my spirit. I do believe I experienced a miracle that afternoon and I came to understand that Jesus did not want me to feel shame and guilt for something that is a natural physiological response to my traumatic memory.

Indeed, it was very painful and traumatic to review my Police Statement yet I felt my spirit was being gently unbound and freed that afternoon. I look forward to further inner healing in the future.

Your experience of Scripture through prayer, visualisation and art

You may like to take some time to journal about how you have experienced this Scripture reading through art and what it has conveyed to you about your own personal journey. This may be helpful to refer back to in the future.

Self-Worth

SELF-WORTH IS ABOUT HOW WE regard ourselves. It depends on how we understand our personal attributes, our strengths, and values. The thermometer for measuring our self-worth is reflected in how we value ourselves.

True self-worth is not based on valuing ourselves for what we have or what we do but for who we are. Self-worth recognises that you are valuable because you are unique; you are you and there is no one else like you in the world.

Unfortunately, when we talk about a person's success, society places greater value on things external to the person rather than the qualities that make a person who they are, such as: love, truthfulness, integrity, compassion, peacefulness, emotional intelligence. This distorted understanding of success leads to a false sense of self-worth. If our determining function of self-worth is based on what society values as successful and not in your inner qualities and values, then our sense of self-worth will be poorly rated.

We can build up our self-worth by discovering our own inner values. For example, you may value *honesty* when asked your opinion, you may value *wholeheartedness* when you give yourself to a project, you may value *taking responsibility* for your actions, you may value *speaking out* when you see injustice, or you may value *generosity* when you see a need. The more we identify our values, the more we build up our self-worth.

Having a true sense of self-worth is so important because it will affect the way we are able to work through challenging situations and, if we should fail at something, how we pick ourselves up to try again.

There are different things that can affect our self-worth. The atmospheres where we live, work, study and socialise can positively or negatively contribute to our self-worth. The way other people treat us and what others say to us can affect our self-worth. However, what affects our self-worth the most is the way we treat ourselves and what we say to ourselves.

Self-Worth

To improve our self-worth, it is so important to get into the habit of constructive self-talk and substituting unhelpful thoughts like, "I'm crap and everything I do is crap", "no one cares about me", with more positive ones like, "I have some good qualities", "I do some things really well", and "There are people who care about me".

As a victim of child sexual abuse, my own self-worth was shattered and it has taken decades to rebuild it. What has worked amazingly well in restoring my self-worth is praying with the Scriptures; that is learning to listen to God speaking to me personally through the Scriptures[86] and being aware that for God I am "precious in his sight, honoured" and God "loves" me[87] and "believes" and "hopes" in me.[88] Making time daily to listen to God in my life has been life-saving as I discovered in prayer a voice that is so much more powerful and able to disperse all my own unhelpful and destructive thoughts.

Prayer is my daily medicine for having a healthy self-worth; I believe it is one of my strongest values for, through it, God has brought out the best in me: hope, love, courage, resilience, life, perseverance, confidence, faith and yes, self-worth.

Below are a variety of beautiful Scripture verses that I would like to share with you; they have contributed to building up my self-worth over the years. They are Scripture verses that can be applied to any context of life that we are living.

The key is to remember, that these are not just Scripture verses written down on a page but behind them is the person of God (in the Jewish Scriptures), and the person of Jesus (in the Christian Scriptures), that is the person who loves us and believes us more than any other person in the world.

It is enough to choose one Scripture verse daily and to practice the steps below that will assist you to replace any unhelpful thoughts with very powerful words that God speaks personally to you. When selecting a Scripture reading, choose one that that is beneficial to your circumstances on a given day, although in my experience, any Word of God/Scripture will always speak to us.

---

86 Documents of the Second Vatican Council, *Dei Verbum, Dogmatic Constitution on Divine Revelation*, #25.
87 Isaiah 43:4a
88 1 Corinthians 13:7

As you practise the steps below on a daily basis, you (and others) will notice that your self-worth is growing stronger and that God is bringing out the best of you.

The Scripture Readings

When you think… "I'm no good! Everything I do is crap"

"God looked at everything he had made and he found it very good."

Genesis 1:31

When you think… "I'm not important… No one cares about me!"

"You are precious in my sight and honoured and I love you."

Isaiah 43:4

"Even if my father and mother forsake me, the Lord will take me in."

Psalm 27:10

"Listen to me… you whom I have upheld since your birth, and have carried since you were born. Even to your old age and grey hairs, I am he who will sustain you. I have made you and I will carry you; I will sustain you and I will rescue you."

Isaiah 46:3b-4

When you think… "I can't do that!"

"Be still and know that I am God!"

Psalm 46:11

When you think… "That's it! It's all too hard! I'm giving up!"

"Choose life, that you and your descendants may live…"

Deuteronomy 30:19

"I know that you can do all things…"

Job 42:2

Self-Worth

"I can do everything through him who gives me strength."

Philippians 4:13

When you think… "I'm falling apart! I'm sinking!"

"My soul clings fast to you; your right hand upholds me."

Psalm 63:9

When you think… "I don't have what it takes! I need to have…"

"The Lord is my shepherd there is nothing I lack.

Psalm 23:1

When you think… "I can't get back up again! I have no more strength"

"Though my flesh and my heart fail, God is the rock of my heart, my portion forever."

Psalm 73:26

"Fear not, I am with you; be not dismayed; I am your God. I will strengthen you and help you, and uphold you with my right hand of justice."

Isaiah 40:10

"God, my Lord, is my strength; he makes my feet swift as those of hinds and enables me to go upon the heights."

Habakkuk 3:19

In green pastures you let me graze; to safe waters you lead me; you restore my strength. You guide me along the right path for the sake of your name."

Psalm 23:2-3

When you think… "I will never be well again!"

"For I will restore you to health; I will heal you of your wounds, says the Lord."

Jeremiah 30:17

When you think… "I can't be forgiven!"

"How could I give you up, O Ephraim (substitute your name), or deliver you up, O Israel (substitute your name)? My heart is overwhelmed, my pity is stirred… I will not destroy Ephraim."

Hosea 11:8-9

"Fear not, you shall not be put to shame; you need not blush, for you shall not be disgraced. The shame of your youth you shall forget."

Isaiah 54:4

"With everlasting kindness I will have compassion on you, says the LORD your Redeemer."

Isaiah 54:8b

When you think… "I have no purpose to exist"

"Before I formed you in the womb, I knew you; before you were born, I called you."

Jeremiah 1:3a

"Listen to me, Jacob, Israel (substitute your name), whom I named! I, it is I who am the first and also the last am I."

Isaiah 48:12

"I will make you a light to the nations…"

Isaiah 49:6

When you think… "I have nothing to look forward to!"

"For I know well the plans I have in mind for you, says the Lord, plans for your welfare and not for your woe, plans to give you a future full of hope."

Jeremiah 29:11

When you think… "Nobody loves me!"

"Love (God's Love for you) is stronger than death… its flames are a blazing

fire. Deep waters cannot quench love (God's love for you), nor floods sweep it away."

Song of Songs 8:6-7

When you catch yourself dwelling on the past...
"Do not remember the events of the past or the things of long ago, See, I am doing something new! Now it springs forth, don't you perceive it?"

Isaiah 43:19

Experiencing the Scripture through Art and Experience of Life
(Suggested materials: an A4 or A3 drawing book, crayons, paints or coloured pencils)

1. Identify an unhelpful thought that is currently recurring for you.
2. Select one of the Scripture readings above that responds positively to this particular unhelpful thought.
3. Take a moment to quieten your thoughts and to be aware of God's Presence in you... Remember, no matter how you are feeling... "God is in this place (space)" even though you may not realise it.[89]
4. Read the Scripture verse(s) slowly, putting your name at the beginning of the phrase or substitute it where for example, "Israel" or "Ephraim" is used and be aware that it is God who is speaking to you through his word.[90] You may want to write this Scripture verse on a fresh page. When you do, put your name at the beginning of the verse to personalise it.
5. Close your eyes and try to gently repeat the words of this Scripture until you feel that you have absorbed God's word and believe it.
6. As you do, you may notice a particular image or symbol that comes to your mind. You may like to draw this image on your page.

---

[89] Part I Hard Places – Sacred Spaces; Genesis 28:16
[90] Documents of the Second Vatican Council, *Dei Verbum, Dogmatic Constitution on Divine Revelation*, #25.

7. What is the significance of the particular image for you? You may want to write that down in a few words on your drawing.
8. Leave your drawing in a place where you can keep coming back to it during the day when you have unhelpful negative thoughts… (in a drawer at work, on your desk at home, on a wall where you can refer to it).
9. During the day, each time the unhelpful thought recurs, return to your page… Recall God's presence in you and then recall the words from Scripture…
10. Close your eyes and repeat the verse(s), trying to absorb God's word until you believe it in your life.
11. After you listen to God's Word, how is it inviting you to think differently about yourself? Others?
12. It could be that God's word is inviting you to do something or behave in a different manner? If so, what can you do? Or how can you behave differently?
13. Whenever the unhelpful thought returns, repeat steps 9-13.

The idea is that each day, you can have a Scripture verse in mind to conquer whatever negative thoughts you are having. By applying the steps above, you will gradually experience a much healthier sense of self-worth.

The Scripture experienced in my life

For a couple of days now, writing has been challenging. As I delve into the issues of this book, chapter by chapter, it has been like opening a can of worms. I begin to feel feelings that I haven't felt for a while, and think things that I haven't thought for a while. I notice at times that my mood changes. I am aware of what is happening; through the writing process my body is remembering the traumatic events from long ago. The emotions and recurring thoughts are ones experienced during that time. It is sometimes painstaking to go through the movements of each chapter and confront the feelings and thoughts that are arising. As I do, I am aware that I am a very different person now to who I was in my past, thanks to my healing journey. I also know that these emotions and thoughts from the past, as real as they are, will eventually pass and who I am now will return.

Lately, I have the recurring thought of feeling, "I am no good! Everything I do is crap!" Every piece of writing that I review I write off as "CRAP!" After reviewing a couple of sections that I wrote off, I become aware that my writing is not the problem but, rather, it is my thoughts that lead me to think, "I am bad and everything I do is crap!" I know that these thoughts are a consequence of my traumatic past and that they have been triggered through the writing process. I know that I must seriously attempt to deal with these distorted thoughts before I write off my whole book as "RUBBISH!"

I stop there where I am in front of my lap top. I take time to become aware of God's presence in me. I open my Bible to Genesis 1:31 and read the words "God looked at everything he had made and he found it *very good*." I replaced the words, "everything" with my name, "Jane" so it read, "God looked at Jane whom he made and he found her very good".

Immediately, I became aware that God was looking at me and saying to me, "Jane, you are very good". I kept repeating the words again and again, believing that through them God was speaking to me and I absorbed them until I believed them with my heart.

I then drew a picture of me in my art journal feeling like crap. Afterwards, I visualised God writing across me in big bold letters, "Jane, you are very good!" There was something about the bigness and boldness of God's letters that spoke to me as if God was saying to me, "Jane, I have the last word, not you!" and I say, "You are very good!" I tried to absorb and believe what God was saying to me.

I then said to God, "Okay, I may be very good but my writing is rubbish!" I re-read the Scripture verse again and this time I understood that God was saying through it, "Your writing is very good!" I would say to God, "No! It's rubbish!" and God said again, "Your writing is very good!" I kept absorbing this word from God until I believed it in my heart.

I then drew on my picture pages of writing scattered around my figure and I kept visualising on each page of writing I had drawn, God writing on them, "It is very good!"

As I reflected on my drawing, it became clear to me that the thoughts I was having were being reflected in the writing I was doing and how important it was to replace those unhelpful thoughts. It also became clear to me how powerful it was to hear from the One who created me, that "I am very good!" No matter what my opinion is of myself, or what others may think of me, to God, "I am very good!" and what I can endeavour to do in life can also be "very good!"

The more I reflected on these thoughts, the more I noticed a change in how I was thinking and feeling about myself. I went back to my writing and re-read what I had reviewed. It was surprising to see how differently I felt about it after working on my thoughts. It wasn't rubbish at all! It was making sense and reflected some very valid points. I could come to appreciate so much more all the effort and hard work that had gone into the writing process.

Stopping to deal with my unhelpful thoughts through the process above made a huge difference to the way I continued with my writing on this particular day. The unhelpful thoughts were a great hindrance to the writing process but once I was able to replace those thoughts with more helpful ones from Scripture, I felt that something from within me unblocked and the creative spirit in me was set free again.

Your experience of Scripture through prayer, visualisation and art

You may like to take some time to journal about how you have experienced this Scripture reading through art and what it has conveyed to you about your own personal journey. This may be helpful to refer back to in the future.

Healthy Silence

"For everything there is a season, and a time for every matter under heaven… A time to keep silence, and a time to speak…"[91]

SURVIVORS OF CHILD SEXUAL ABUSE are well acquainted with "unhealthy" silence and its devastating impacts and effects. For thousands of survivors in Australia, the announcement of the Royal Commission into Institutional Responses to Child Sexual Abuse (RCIRCSA)[92] signified a "time to speak" and to finally break the "unhealthy" silence that had been painfully borne for decades. The reality, however, is that there are still many who haven't spoken out because they may not have felt the strength and courage to come forward. It may still take decades before they find the courage to tell their stories.

Understandably, for survivors who have been forcefully silenced for decades, experiencing any type of "silence" can be painstaking because it reminds us of our traumatic past. Consequently, trying to comprehend how silence can be "healthy" is challenging. Silence is a very powerful form of communication and while its "unhealthy" use can cause pain, hurt and even harm to others, if it is used in the right way, it can transform conversations and relationships. Learning to practise "healthy" silence is a useful and effective communication skill but it means overcoming negative experiences of "unhealthy" silence.

Generally, we understand silence to mean the absence of speech. However, if a person isn't speaking it doesn't mean they're not communicating. Research conducted by Dr Albert Mehrabian revealed that words convey only seven percent of our message, while ninety-three percent of our communication is non-verbal and occurs through tone, volume, facial expressions, gestures,

---

[91] Ecclesiastes 3:1;7b
[92] In November 2012, Prime Minister Julia Gillard announced a Royal Commission into Institutional Responses to Child Sexual Abuse to investigate institutional child sexual abuse in Australia. The work of the RCIRCSA was extended to December 2017 and by March 2017, 6,500 survivors had come forward to tell their stories in both private and public hearings with 2,000 still on the waiting list to tell their stories.

posture and the like.[93] Seemingly, the greater part of what we communicate is silent.

So how can silence be "healthy"?

First, a healthy silence leads to personal growth. The silent gap between talking in conversations enables us to absorb what has been said into our spirit. By practising this form of silence in conversations, we learn to communicate from a deeper place within ourselves. Some of the questions that one may ask in those reflective moments of silence are: Do I believe what I just said? Is it really how I feel/think? Why did I just say that? Did I respond to what was just said? This process of reflecting moves to self-discovery and, consequently, growth takes place.

Secondly, healthy silence within a confrontational conversation may catalyse a turning point. Gaps of silence can be like pressing the "pause" button that allows engagement in self-reflection. As a result, one's thinking may change completely. It may also be an effective means for reducing tension and dissipating intense emotions that may arise. If skilfully used, silence can completely turn around and transform confrontational conversations.

Some people also experience that silence is helpful because it provides a space for them to apply techniques such as counting to ten; or deep breathing which may dissolve tension.

In conversations, silence can also be a very powerful tool that enables authentic and mutual soul-searching to take place so that to the deeper truth of 'who we are' is communicated and brought to light.

Using silence in these ways empowers us particularly when conversations are confrontational and challenging.

If we turn to the Scriptures, we find examples of Jesus practising "healthy" silence within the context of some of the most challenging and confrontational conversations he had with the religious and civil authorities.

You may find something striking in these conversations that you would like to develop and practise in your own conversations as a means of communicating more effectively.

---

93   Albert Mehrabian is currently Professor Emeritus of Psychology, UCLA. He is most well-known for his publications on the relative importance of verbal and nonverbal messages

The Scripture Reading

The following Scripture verses demonstrate Jesus practising a healthy silence, particularly in difficult and challenging conversations and confrontations.

In a heated confrontation with the Scribes and Pharisees, Jesus combines healthy silence, body language and creative expression through writing:

> They said to him, "Teacher, this woman was caught in the very act of committing adultery. Now in the law Moses commanded us to stone such women. Now what do you say?" They said this to test him, so that they might have some charge to bring against him. Jesus bent down and wrote with his finger on the ground. When they kept on questioning him, he straightened up and said to them, "Let anyone among you who is without sin be the first to throw a stone at her." And once again he bent down and wrote on the ground. When they heard it, they went away, one by one, beginning with the elders; and Jesus was left alone with the woman standing before him.
>
> John 8:4b-9

If we imagine ourselves as onlookers to this scene, we may imagine a very tense and hostile atmosphere created by the Scribes and Pharisees and directed towards the woman and Jesus. When the Scribes and Pharisees bring this woman before Jesus their intention was "to test him, so that they may have a charge to bring against him". When they questioned Jesus initially, he was silent and "bent down and wrote with his finger on the ground". We do not know how long Jesus remained writing on the ground but what's important is that he was silent while the Scribes and Pharisees "kept questioning him". When Jesus eventually straightens up and answers them, his response challenges their thinking and their behaviour, "Let anyone among you who is without sin be the first to throw a stone at her". After saying this again, Jesus is silent and bends down and writes on the ground. The Scribes and Pharisees walk away one by one and no one casts a stone.

It is an extraordinary example of "healthy" silence being used skilfully and effectively. Through silence, and in the heat of the moment, Jesus presses the "pause" button as a means of inviting the Scribes and Pharisees to engage in self-reflection. Perhaps whatever Jesus wrote on the ground was an extension of this invitation. Amazingly, the use of silence effectively and completely changed their thinking and behaviour. Also, the silence has completely dissolved the tension and intense hostility. It is a powerful example of how silence can completely turn around and transform conversations.

The following scriptural verses are in the context of the "Passion narratives", that is, they are gospel accounts referring to Jesus' suffering (from his agony and arrest in Gethsemane) leading up to his death and burial.

Jesus silent before the High Priest and the council:

> *Now the chief priests and the whole council were looking for false testimony against Jesus so that they might put him to death, but they found none, though many false witnesses came forward. At last two came forward and said, "This fellow said, 'I am able to destroy the temple of God and build it in three days.'" The high priest stood up and said, "Have you no answer? What is it that they testify against you?" But Jesus was silent.*
>
> Matthew 26:59-63a

Jesus silent before Pilate:

> *They bound Jesus, led him away, and handed him over to Pilate. Pilate asked him, "Are you the King of the Jews?" He answered him, "You say so." Then the chief priests accused him of many things. Pilate asked him again, "Have you no answer? See how many charges they bring against you?" But Jesus made no further reply, so that Pilate was amazed.*
>
> Mark 15:1b-5

In the verses from the Gospel of Matthew, Jesus has been arrested and brought before the religious authorities who "were looking for false testimony against him so that they might put him to death". They are not open to the truth of who Jesus said he is – the Son of God. They listen to witness after witness but cannot find the evidence they need to arrest him. Finally, two witnesses come forward testifying that Jesus said, "I am able to destroy the temple of God and build it in three days."[94] Although the testimony of the witnesses is true, when asked by the high priest "Have you no answer? What is it they testify against you", Jesus is silent.

In the verses from the Gospel of Mark, Jesus is brought before Pilate.

Throughout the testimonies in both, Jesus practises a long sustained silence. In the verses from Matthew's Gospel, perhaps Jesus' silence after the initial evidence meant that what was said did not amount to anything worth a reply. He remains silent after the final two testimonies because the evidence presented was true so there was nothing to be said.

Perhaps Jesus intended to be silent as a means of allowing the truth of what the witnesses had said to be absorbed into the spirit of the Scribes and Pharisees, moving them to engage in a self-reflective process as happened in John 8:4b-9.

However, by this stage, silence was pointless because the Scribes and Pharisees had already made up their minds and decided Jesus' tragic fate.

Yet, we cannot underestimate the power of Jesus' silence. Perhaps in that gap of silence, there may have been one person in that council who may have engaged in the self-reflective process asking the question, "Why can't I believe this? Why is it so troubling for me to hear? If it's true, what is it challenging in me?"

When survivors finally find the strength to tell our truth, we do not always get a response we like. In fact, often enough, the initial responses may be very confronting and challenging. Some people may ask us very specific details and question us repeatedly. Some people may be generous in their defences towards the perpetrator making us feel like a liar. Some people may decide as soon as we come out with the truth that, "It can't be true!" and "I don't want it to be true!"

Gaps of "healthy" silence in these conversations may be helpful. Allow spaces as Jesus did for the other party to listen to and absorb into their spirit what they have just said to you or asked; spaces where they can be self-reflective and discover within them, "Why can't I believe this? Why is it so troubling for me to hear? If it's true, what is it challenging in me?"

---

94   Matthew 24:2; Matthew 27:40

Even though they may not change their thinking and turn around to support you, don't underestimate your attempt to practise "healthy" silence. We may not experience the effect in the first, second or third conversation but over time, your gaps of silence may eventually invite them to enter into a self-reflective process.

Jesus silent before Pilate

> *Pilate asked Jesus,"So you are a king?" Jesus answered,"You say I am a king. For this I was born, and for this I came into the world, to testify to the truth. Everyone who belongs to the truth listens to my voice." Pilate asked him,"What is truth?"*
>
> John 18:37-38

There is no recorded response from Jesus to Pilate's question, "What is truth?" but one might imagine Jesus remaining silent, allowing Pilate to assimilate in his spirit what he has just asked Jesus. The silence of Jesus was provoking some real soul-searching in Pilate.

Perhaps when others are asking us for the truth repeatedly, even though we have told them repeatedly, it may be effective to practise "healthy" silence. Perhaps by simply standing silently in our truth, as Jesus did before Pilate, the other may do some deep soul-searching asking themselves, "What is truth?"

Experiencing the Scripture through art and experience of life
(Suggested materials: an A4 or A3 drawing book, crayons, paints or coloured pencils)

1. You may like to title your page: Healthy Silence.
2. Take some time to quieten your thoughts and to be aware of God's Presence in you... Remember, no matter how you are feeling... "God is in this place (space)" even though you may not realise it.[95]

---

[95] Part I Hard Places – Sacred Spaces; Genesis 28:16

Healthy Silence

3. Take time to read the Scripture verse(s) slowly. Try to visualise yourself as an onlooker in these confrontations between Jesus and the religious and civil authorities.
4. What is it that calls your attention as you visualise this scene?
5. Take time to notice how Jesus is silent. Are there questions arising in your heart that you would like to ask Jesus? For example, Why were you silent Jesus? Why didn't you defend yourself? What was the purpose of your silence? Take time to ask Jesus.
6. Are you able to listen to God responding in your spirit? What do you understand God is saying to you about "silence" as you read these verses from Scripture?[96]
7. Does this change your belief around "silence" in any way? If so, how? You may want to write this on your page, expressing what you are saying, with colours.
8. As you read these verses from Scripture, perhaps you started thinking around conversations you may like to have in the future that you sense will be challenging and confronting.
9. Try to spend time visualising that scene in the future. Who would be present? Where you may like to have that conversation?
10. Begin a new page in your art journal and title it "Healthy Silence". Divide the page in half.
11. On the left hand side - spend time drawing the scene you have visualised (remember, it's not about drawing perfect figures... it's about creatively expressing what you carry within your spirit).
    i) Are you able to sum up in words what you would like to say? You may want to write this around the figure representing you on your drawing.
    ii) How do you visualise the other person(s) responding to what you say? You may want to sum it up in words around their figures on your drawing.

---

[96] Documents of the Second Vatican Council, *Dei Verbum, Dogmatic Constitution on Divine Revelation*, #25.

12. Would you consider using silence as a tool in your conversation? At what point in the conversation would you use "silence"? What would be your intention in using silence?
13. On the right hand side of your page, visualise how the scene may look in silence… Represent each person on your drawing including yourself.
    i) What effect would you like silence to have on the person(s) present? Can you represent this on your drawing…? (Write words if it is easier.)
    ii) What would you like them to absorb into their spirits from what you will say to them?
    iii) What questions would you like them to ask themselves as they reflect during the silence? (You may want to write these around their figures on your drawing.)
    iv) What outcome would you like to see silence producing in them? (You may want to write this on your picture.)
    v) What is it that you would like to communicate in the silence (through your body language ….) to those present? (You may want to represent this on your drawing).
    vi) What are the sorts of emotions that may arise that you believe silence can reduce or dissolve? (You may want to represent this on your drawing.)

You may like to come back to this drawing before you have this conversation and allow it to remind you about developing the skill of "healthy" silence in your conversation.

You may have experienced that it was beneficial for you to visualise and draw a challenging conversation that you need to have in the future and what it may look like. If so, you may like to work through this activity in the future before having a challenging conversation and also be reminded about using the skill of healthy silence.

The Scripture experienced in my life

In 2018, after the Royal Commission into Institutional Responses to Child Sexual Abuse had its final public hearing investigating The Catholic Church, shocking statistics were released, revealing the number of religious priests, brothers, sisters and lay people who have had claims of sexual abuse against them. This received widespread media coverage.

While large numbers of Catholics feel rocked by such alarming numbers and heads are hung in shame, surprisingly, I have met the occasional "Catholic" who still defends the Church on this issue and believes that, "the Church couldn't have done such grave harm!" and "It can't possibly be as bad as the media says it is!". Rather than seeing the RCIRCSA's investigations into the Catholic Church as a call to responsibility and accountability, their belief is that "the Church is being targeted" or "persecuted" by the RCIRCSA.

I had a very casual and unplanned encounter with one of "these" Catholics during this time. After we said our "hellos", one of the first things she commented about was "how unjust" it was that "again" the Catholic Church was being "scrutinised" by the RCIRSCA.

I looked at her and stayed silent with the intention that she might be self-reflective and hear what she had just said. She looked at me and waited for me to say something. After my initial silence, I asked her, "Is it just for a member of the clergy to violate a vulnerable child's innocence?" Then again, I stayed silent.

I had hoped that she could absorb my question into her spirit. She looked at me dumbfounded and was briefly silent. After a pause of silence, she simply said, "That can never be right!" I noticed a change in her body posture… Her self-righteous posture seemed to change to one that reflected humiliation. I wanted to leave the conversation there so that she could hear what she had just said and reflect further. I excused myself to continue with my errands and said goodbye. The lady did not know that I am a survivor of clergy child sexual abuse.

I do not know if this lady's stance changed towards the work of the RCIRCSA and the inquiries into the Catholic Church but through our interaction what became evident to me was the effectiveness of "silence" when it is used as a means for self-reflection and shifting feelings.

I believe that "healthy" silence is empowering, particularly for survivors of child sexual abuse who may find themselves in conversations where the truth is not believed and strongly disputed, and when asked for proof or evidence.

I hope to continue developing and incorporating the skill of "healthy" silence into my conversations in the future.

Your experience of Scripture through prayer, visualisation and art

You may like to take some time to journal about how you have experienced this Scripture reading through art and what it has conveyed to you about your own personal journey. This may be helpful to refer back to in the future.

Facing Fear

IN THE NEXT COUPLE OF days, I have an appointment with the detective who is working with the Department of Public Prosecution's Office to prepare for the Trial of the Accused. She has asked if I can make a further formal Statement about some evidence that has emerged.

As the day of my appointment draws closer, fear begins to arise in me. I need to stop my thoughts from running ahead to the time of the Trial where I find myself thinking, "If I have this fear now, what will I be like when the Trial comes!" However, I have learnt that the best way to deal with this lengthy and painstaking prosecution process (going on to five years now) is "to take one day at a time" doing my best to live each day as fully as possible.

Coming forward and speaking out means facing fear. Even though it is now three decades since I was sexually abused, the fear that was instilled in me; during the grooming process, while I was being sexually abused, and post sexual abuse, surfaces in me again and threatens to overpower me. I can nearly hear the voice of my perpetrator re-sounding in my ears again, "If you say anything to anyone, I will find out and I will kill you!" What I am currently experiencing is what any survivor who comes forward experiences – re-traumatisation[97]. It is the cost of coming forward and one of the reasons why victims of sexual abuse may choose not to speak out.

The other great fear of speaking out is the fear of not being believed and being told, "It can't be true! Everyone knows that he/she is such a wonderful person!" Or, "Could you be imagining it?" Or, "I've noticed you haven't been well for a while!" (Implying that we may have a mental disorder that is making us imagine such things.)

Consequent to this lies the fear of being rejected or shunned by family or friends and finding ourselves totally alone.

In both the Hebrew and Christian Scriptures of the Bible, we are encouraged

---

97 A relapse into a state of trauma triggered by a some subsequent event.

continually not to be afraid. Fear is what holds us back from doing good for ourselves and for others.

Jesus encourages us not to be afraid to come forward and do good by speaking out! He encourages us to face our fear because he did it himself. He came forward and spoke out against many injustices that he saw not only in the religious but also the civil systems. He spoke out for the exploited, ignored, mistreated, enslaved, abused, objectified and the despised.

Jesus faced his fear to such a degree that he wasn't afraid to disrupt social norms, anger the religious leaders, criticise the governments and condemn officials.

Whenever wrong is done, Jesus encourages us not to be afraid to reveal it. Institutions and systems can only change wrong to right if there are people brave enough to come forward and speak out. This means facing fear.

Both the Hebrew and Christian Scriptures contain many verses where God invites us not to be afraid. I have included some here that you may find helpful. You may like to work through the suggested steps in "Experiencing the Scripture" as a way of facing your own fear.

You may find that a particular Scripture verse will speak to you more on one day than it might on another. The multiple verses provided gives you the opportunity to re-visit the verses whenever you experience fear, and to work with the one that resonates most with you.

Scripture Readings

Fear not, Abram! (Substitute your name here for "Abram") I am your shield; I will make your reward very great.

Genesis 15:1

Be brave and steadfast, have no fear or dread of them, for it is the Lord, your God, who marches with you, he will never fail or forsake you.

Deuteronomy 31:6

Facing Fear

Fear not, I am with you; be not dismayed; I am your God. I will strengthen you and help you, and uphold you with my right hand of justice.
Isaiah 40:10

For I am the Lord your God who grasps your right hand; it is I who say to you, 'Fear not, I will help you.'
Isaiah 40:13

Fear not, you shall not be put to shame; you need not blush, for you shall not be disgraced. The shame of your youth you shall forget.
Isaiah 54:4

But now says the Lord who created you... Do not be afraid for I have redeemed you; I have called you by name: you are mine. When you pass through water, I will be with you; in the rivers you shall not drown. When you walk through fire, you shall not be burned; the flames shall not consume you. For I am the Lord, your God.
Isaiah 43:1-2

Do not fear the king of Babylon (substitute "king of Babylon" with the name of the person you fear), before whom you are now afraid, do not fear him, says the Lord, for I am with you to save you, to rescue you from his power.
Jeremiah 42:11

The Lord, your God, who goes before you, will himself fight for you...
Deuteronomy 1:29

Fear not, Jerusalem! He who gave you your name is your encouragement. Fearful are those who harmed you, who rejoiced at your downfall.
Baruch 4:30-31

Fear not, beloved, you are safe; take courage and be strong.
Daniel 10:19

Fear not, O Zion (substitute your name for "Zion"), be not discouraged! The Lord, your God, is in your midst, a mighty saviour.

Zephaniah 3:16

The Lord is with me, I am not afraid!

Psalm 118:6

Immediately he spoke to them and said, 'Take courage! It is I. Don't be afraid.

Mark 6:50

Jesus told him, 'Don't be afraid; just believe.

Mark 5:36

And I am convinced that nothing can ever separate us from God's love. Neither death nor life, neither angels nor demons, neither our fears for today nor our worries about tomorrow – not even the powers of hell can separate us from God's love.

Romans 8:38-39

Don't be afraid, I am with you.

Matthew 28:20

Experiencing the Scripture through prayer, visualisation and art
(Suggested materials: an A4 or A3 drawing book, crayons, paints or coloured pencils)

1. Take some time to be aware of God's presence with you.
2. Read through the Scripture readings slowly then choose one reading that you would like to work with to face your fear.
3. Re-read the Scripture reading slowly, putting your name at the beginning of the phrase.

Facing Fear

4. Is there a particular word that resonates with you? What does this word(s) evoke in you or how do you react to these words?
5. You may like to have a conversation with God around these words, asking questions or sharing your thoughts. For example, if the words, "Don't be afraid!" strike you, you may want to express what you really feel to God... "God, I am afraid! I am afraid that...." Or, "I am afraid of...."
6. After you have expressed what you truly feel to God, re-read the words of Scripture slowly absorbing them into your spirit.
7. On a new page in your Art Journal put the title: Facing Fear.
8. When you read this verse today, was there a particular event that came to your mind? (That is, an event or situation that is approaching and that you are fearful of, or a recurring event that provokes fear in you.)
9. Take some time to visualise what that scene might look like.
10. Take some time now to draw the scene you have visualised.
    i) Can you name your fears in a few words (you may want to write those words on your picture)?
11. Take some time now to re-visualise the scene with God in it.
12. Draw what the scene looks like with God in it?
13. After you have drawn God in your scene, what do you notice about it (for example, maybe you have drawn God bigger than everyone and everything in the scene... this might mean that you visualise God overpowering everyone and everything, or perhaps you have drawn God very close to you... this might mean that God is closer to you than you imagine)?
14. How is the scene with God in it different to the one you visualised beforehand?
15. Has visualising the scene increased your courage?
16. You may want to write the words from the Scripture verse on your drawing.

If you feel bold enough, you may like to set a day or time to face the particular fear that you have worked with today. Before you attempt the challenge, come back to this picture and visualise the scene. Remember, God will be present and encourage you not to be afraid in the same way that you have visualised God in your drawing. Whenever you feel your fear arising, keep bringing these words of Scripture to mind.

The Scripture experienced in my life

Don't be afraid, I am with you.

Matthew 28:20

As a preparation for my appointment with the detective, I made some time to work with the fear that was arising in me.

I was aware that I was re-living the same feelings that I experienced at the time of the trauma: fear, dismay, powerlessness, and helplessness. It was as if the ground was opening up beneath me.

I read through the Scripture verses one by one. The verse from the Gospel of Matthew 28:20 struck me. I re-read the verse slowly several times putting my name at the beginning of the phrase.

As I read these words, I felt they were spoken to me by someone who knew me very well so it wasn't necessary to say anything, and someone who loved me so much that their unconditional presence was guaranteed even without me having to ask for it. What I felt was true – Jesus knows me and loves me! Jesus knew I was afraid, and he also knew that I would only get through this with a presence that was bigger and mightier than any human presence.

I spoke to Jesus honestly about my fears. My mind was racing at one hundred miles per hour. I put to him all my "What ifs…? What if I get so frightened that I paralyse? What if they ask me to do something I feel I am not strong enough to do? What if we don't finish everything we need to do during the appointment time and I need to go back again?" Jesus had only one response for everything I put to him, "Don't be afraid, I am with you."

For my hundred "what ifs", Jesus responded with one hundred affirmations – "Don't be afraid, I am with you!" The affirmations were assuring and consoling.

I pulled out my art journal. I visualised the scene of my appointment and drew it. My drawing was very simple. There were two figures, one that represented myself, and the other, the detective. In between us I drew a desk. It was interesting that I drew myself so much smaller than the detective. I believe it is symbolic of how small and helpless I am feeling in the process of prosecution and lead up to the trial. It was also interesting that I drew a dark outline around myself. I believe the "darkness" symbolised the fear. I noticed that I didn't draw the detective so.

I then re-visualised the scene with Jesus in it… and drew it as I had visualised it. I wrote the words "Don't be afraid, I am with you". What I had drawn surprised me. I had drawn Jesus around my own figure so that it looked like I was one with Jesus (inside his figure). Jesus' figure was so much bigger than my figure. His colours were radiant and warm… and I seemed to be absorbed in them so that the dark outline around my figure dissolved. The whole colour of the room changed with the presence of Jesus.

As I looked at my picture; it had a powerful effect in me. It affirmed Jesus' loving care of me and his divine power to disperse all my fears.

This afternoon I received the gift of God's grace that guaranteed me the confidence to face my fears through the power of God's Word.

Listening to God's Word in prayer, visualising it and expressing it in art form is a wonderfully gentle and transformative way to heal.

Your experience of Scripture through prayer, visualisation and art

You may like to take some time to journal about how you have experienced this Scripture reading through art and what it has conveyed to you about your own personal journey. This may be helpful to refer back to in the future.

Believing without Seeing

THE PROCESS OF HEALING FROM childhood sexual abuse is life-long. Just as we seem to experience we are getting a better handle on one issue, a new one, perhaps even more challenging than the previous emerges, or an old one may reappear (through an event or circumstances in our life) with yet another new and deeper layer that requires peeling back. At least, this is how I experience my journey that began neraly three decades ago.

Life after the trauma of sexual abuse is never impact free. Even though the quality of life may gradually improve as healing and transformation takes place, there will always be impacts to deal with. Sadly, the work involved in a process of healing from childhood sexual abuse is often not understood or appreciated. This is reflected back to survivors when they are told things like, "Why don't you just get over it!" or "It's time to move on!" If only it were that easy! If only we could get over all the issues that are part of the "package" in a couple of hours and not have to deal with it ever again! If only we can move forward and live our life not having to deal with our past coming back to us every day in one way or another!

But the reality is that the damage and grave harm caused from sexual abuse cuts so deeply to the core of its victim that it is impossible for it to be repaired overnight. It cannot be repaired in a single sitting of telling our story and being heard, or in one session of psychotherapy, or in one letter or email confronting the perpetrator or the Institution responsible, or in one visit to the police. The reality is that from the day that the abuse took place, the victim's life is changed forever; life after this trauma becomes a quest to survive what has happened to us by learning to live with and heal the impacts and effects of sexual abuse.

Getting "over" sexual abuse and "moving on" is a process that happens over time. Although survivors would like to deal with all the impacts at once, it's impossible. Each issue needs to be dealt with individually and no one can predict how long it will take to heal an individual issue. How can you predict the time it will take someone who has been sexually abused, to experience the world as a safe place again, or to see a Church or religious symbol without getting angry,[98] or to trust again, or to find their voice again? Some issues may feel like they will never be completely healed although we may have conscientiously "worked" with the issue. The reality is that healing from sexual abuse is a life-long process.

The journey of healing for survivors can feel like riding a roller-coaster. There are lots of ups and downs along the way. One day, we feel we are doing well but the next day we are in despair. One day, we feel we are moving forwards but the next day we feel we've gone so far backwards. One day, we feel we are becoming sane but the next day we feel we are going insane.

It is understandable why survivors who are working towards healing will often find themselves questioning "why?": "Why am I going through all this pain?", "What am I gaining from this process?", "How is this process fruitful?", "What evidence do I have that it's beneficial for me?" It can feel like we are investing so much of ourselves into working with our issues and doing it to the best of our capacity but nothing seems to be happening, that is, we feel we are not changing.

It is so hard to believe that working with our issues is benefitting us when we don't see the fruit of our work. We don't mind investing ourselves if it means seeing the fruit of our work! We don't mind doing a week's work as long as it means payment at the end of the week. We don't mind spending hours studying if it means a satisfactory exam result. We don't mind dieting and sacrificing food we like if it means losing extra kilos. We don't mind spending time preparing a meal if it means seeing family and friends enjoy it. As long as we see the fruit of our work, we don't mind investing ourselves.

But when it comes to working with our issues of sexual abuse, often what we find ourselves dealing with are spiritual issues, meaning issues that relate to the human spirit rather than material or physical things – we are dealing with things that are not tangible but are essential for life and relationships - things like a sense of safety, trust, the courage to come forward, acceptance.

Because we are working with spiritual issues, "seeing" the fruit of our work is even more challenging because it happens over time. Whilst I can ask someone

---

98   Referring to if the sexual abuse was by a member of the clergy

a question and get an immediate answer, or turn on a light switch and get instant light, the realization of spiritual things takes time, especially when one has been wounded spiritually! It takes time to feel safe, it takes time to re-build trust, it takes time to develop courage, it takes time to come to acceptance. If we don't sense in "this time" that change is happening because cannot see the fruit of our work in our life, then the temptation is to give up and lose hope!

The challenge on our healing journey is to believe that as long as we are working with our issues, we are being changed and transformed even though we may not see the fruit of our work. It's an invitation to "believe without seeing".

If we are able to work through our issues with this faith, at a time when we least expect it, and through God's grace, we will see the abundant fruit of all our hard work.

As we read in the letter to the Hebrews, "Now faith means putting our full confidence in the things we hope for; it means being certain of things we cannot see."[99]

You may find the Scripture reading below helpful, especially during the times that you are tempted to give up, believing that healing and transformation is taking place within you.

The Scripture Reading

When it was evening on that day, the first day of the week, and the doors of the house where the disciples had met were locked for fear of the Jews, Jesus came and stood among them and said, "Peace be with you." After he said this, he showed them his hands and his side. Then the disciples rejoiced when they saw the Lord. But Thomas (who was called the Twin), one of the twelve, was not with them when Jesus came. So the other disciples told him, "We have seen the Lord." But he said to them, "Unless I see the mark of the nails in his hands, and put my finger in the mark of the nails and my hand in his side, I will not believe." A week later his disciples were again in the house, and Thomas was with them. Although the doors were shut, Jesus came and stood among them and said, "Peace be with you." Then he said to Thomas, "Put your

---

99 Hebrews 1:11

finger here and see my hands. Reach out your hand and put it in my side. Do not doubt but believe." Thomas answered him, "My Lord and my God!" Jesus said to him, "Have you believed because you have seen me? Blessed are those who have not seen and yet have come to believe."

John 20:19-21; 24-29

This story from Scripture is one of a collection of gospel stories that make up the Resurrection narratives.[100]

Prior to this Scripture, the disciples have already heard from Mary that she had seen Jesus alive.[101] This message hadn't sunk in yet for the disciples who, in this scene, are behind locked doors because they are afraid of the Jews who knew they were Jesus' most intimate friends. They may have been thinking, "It's just a matter of time until they come looking for us!"

What a surprise it must have been when Jesus suddenly appeared standing right there in front of them and wishing them, "Peace!" I imagine a myriad of thoughts ran through their minds like, "Who is this among us? How on earth did he get in when the doors are locked? Can it be Jesus? It's the greeting he would greet us with but he's supposed to be dead!?" I imagine they were all very startled by this sudden appearance.

Perhaps this is the reason why Jesus first offers them, "Peace!" – "Peace!" to calm their fear, "Peace!" to ease their grief, "Peace!" to soothe their guilt, "Peace!" for healing.

Even though the greeting may have sounded familiar and as if it was coming from Jesus they were probably thinking, "How could it be possible that he is alive after suffering such a traumatic and tragic death?"

Jesus sees them struggling to believe so he shows them his hands and side. Then, after seeing this, the disciples "rejoice". The penny finally drops and they realise they are in the presence of the glorified Lord who has conquered death and been raised to Life. I am sure they were amazed because although Jesus was bodily present to them, his new life was beyond human limitation and no longer bound by space and time. Jesus can now enter through walls and closed doors! The risen Jesus exists in a new form. Life for Jesus has not ended, but changed.

---

100   The Resurrection narratives are the gospel accounts of Jesus rising from the dead.
101   John 20:18

No wonder they "rejoiced"! First, their friend who they were grieving was alive! Secondly, if he was there alive with them, it meant that death is not the end, but the beginning of a new and transformed life.

The message that Jesus invites us to believe through this Scripture is one of great hope. None of us can escape the final act of physical death but, before we arrive there, we face many "spiritual" deaths along the way. No one is immune to them. Every time we suffer any kind of loss: a person we love, an aspect of our health, a job, a house, a place where we love living; we experience spiritual death and we feel grief, sadness, anger, and that something meaningful to us has been lost. Due to the multiple impacts of sexual abuse, survivors are constantly dealing with losses: loss of trust, loss of innocence, loss of self-esteem, loss of having a voice, loss of being in control, loss of faith, loss of meaning, loss of family or friends (if we are not believed), loss of mental capacity/ability, loss of career… No matter how long the list is of losses suffered and how traumatic and tragic these spiritual deaths are for us, through this Scripture Jesus invites us not to lose hope and to believe that these deaths are not the end for us but rather the beginning of new life and transformation. Like Jesus, our life will not end in these "spiritual deaths" (even though it may feel like it at times) but we will be changed and transformed into a "new" person with "new" life if we believe in the power of the Resurrection.

What a magnificent evening this would have been for Jesus' disciples! One that would have stayed etched in their memories for the rest of their life. I imagine a memory that they may have brought to mind everytime they were tempted to lose hope in the fate of spiritual challenges.

But Thomas missed out on the appearance of Jesus and even though the other ten disciples were telling him, "We have seen the Lord!", Thomas could not believe it… Would you blame him? If someone said to me that a person who had died last week came back to life and visited them, I think I would also react like Thomas and not believe it! Thomas insisted, *"Unless I see the mark of the nails in his hands, and put my finger in the mark of the nails and my hand in his side, I will not believe"*. Thomas couldn't believe without seeing. He wanted to experience for himself that Jesus was alive!

Believing without Seeing

That experience wasn't granted to Thomas immediately but it came to him a week later when the disciples were in exactly the same scenario of being behind "locked doors". Again, Jesus appears to them and offers them "Peace!" Aware of Thomas' desire to "see" for himself so that he can believe, Jesus gifts him a unique experience. Not only does Jesus show Thomas his wounded body but he invites him to, *"Put your finger here and see my hands. Reach out your hand and put it in my side."* I wonder if Thomas might have experienced an ounce of trepidation as he reached out to touch Jesus' wounds, perhaps already sensing what this was implying for his own life – a call to believe that there is transformation and new life even after the most traumatic death! How privileged Thomas would have felt to have been given this unique experience by Jesus!

Jesus then invites Thomas, *"Do not doubt but believe"*.

Jesus speaks the same words to us through God's word, "Do not doubt but believe". These are the words that we are invited to listen to repeatedly when we doubt. For example: We doubt we can't be different and think, "I will always be like this! I can't be different. This is how I am!" We doubt that even though we are working hard at our issues, things are shifting, moving and being transformed within us through the very same power and grace that raised Jesus to new life.[102] We doubt that there is a future full of hope to look forward to[103]. We doubt that coming forward will make a difference for us and others in some way. We doubt that having a voice can create change in us, others and in the dysfunctional systems where we were harmed. Each of us can make our own list of doubts. But if we share each one of our doubts with Jesus, he will respond through God's word, "Do not doubt but believe".

With his own eyes, Thomas "saw" Jesus changed in his presence. He saw that his wounds were no longer raw and hurting but healed and transformed. Jesus was new. Thomas saw and believed. It was a turning point for Thomas: his disbelief is turned around to belief, his losing hope is turned around to hope, his

---

102   1 Corinthians 15:52 "It will happen in a moment, in the blink of an eye, when the last trumpet is blown. For when the trumpet sounds, those who have died will be raised to live forever. And we who are living will also be transformed."

103   Jeremiah 29:11 "For surely I know the plans I have for you, says the Lord, plans for your welfare and not for harm, to give you a future with hope."

disappointment is turned around to blessing and his faith is turned around as he acknowledges Jesus to be, "My Lord and my God!"

Although this experience was a gift of God's grace to Thomas, Jesus then says to him, "Have you believed because you have seen me? Blessed are those who have not seen and yet have come to believe."

It's natural for us, like Thomas, to want to see first and then believe but Jesus promises us if we believe without seeing, we will be blessed.

Blessed with what? Blessed with the experience that the tragedy and trauma of sexual abuse is not the end for us! Yes, certainly our life is not as it was before but as we work through our issues towards healing, our life is changed through the same power and grace of the risen Jesus who lives with us. Through grace, new life slowly begins to emerge again and we are blessed with abundant spiritual gifts during the process: peace, courage, trust, love, strength, resilience, acceptance, wisdom, compassion, gentleness.

In this Resurrection story, the risen Jesus reflects back to us our own story of trauma and tragedy. Like him, we too bear wounds and we live with the impacts of these wounds. But Jesus invites us to cast our belief on the greater Truth; the truth that these wounds are not the end of the story for us and to believe that there is an even better ending yet to come but already in progress as we work through our issues even though we can't see it yet.

This Scripture is an invitation to believe that there IS life beyond a traumatic past; like the risen Jesus, we too will be restored and made new. Change and transformation is taking place within our lives even though we may not see the fruit of our work. New life will begin to emerge for us just as it did for the risen Jesus.

So remarkable was this new life in Jesus that even those closest to him had trouble recognising him. Even though there was clear evidence of the things that identified him like his wounds, he was different! He was transformed and changed.

This is the hope we can hold on to as we continue to move forward… Our story of tragedy will always be the same but if we believe in the power of Jesus' Resurrection working within us, we will be changed and transformed in ways beyond our imaginings.

Experiencing the Scripture through prayer, visualisation and reflection on Art Journal.
(You will need your Art Journal.)

1. Take some time to still yourself within; and be aware of God's presence with you.
2. Read through the Scripture reading slowly, trying to imagine the scene. If you can, in the first part of the reading, visualise yourself as one of the disciples, and in the second part of the reading, visualise yourself as Thomas.
    i) Notice how you react when Jesus appears in the room.
    ii) Notice how you react when Jesus shows you his wounds.[104] Try to allow Jesus' wounds to reflect back to you your own story of trauma. What are you understanding as Jesus shows you his wounds?
    iii) When Jesus invites you to "touch" his wounds, notice how you react.[105] (Do you resist, are you afraid, open to the invitation, angry, disgusted...?) You may want to express to Jesus what you are experiencing.
    iv) Touching Jesus' wounds is like touching and feeling

---

[104] The invitation to "look at" Jesus' wounds may stir up traumatic memories associated with the perpetrator so I will leave it to the survivor to discern if they feel up to continuing with this activity or not. In the case that you would like to continue the activity and experience painful memories or flashbacks, you may find that working through the following steps is helpful in overcoming some of the spiritual impacts that the sexual abuse has had on your relating to God: 1. Was there a particular thought that came to your mind or did you experience a flashback? 2. As this came to you, what were you feeling? (Anxiety, fear, terror...) 3. Try to identify who these thoughts, flashbacks, or feelings refer to (for example, your perpetrator). 4. Once you have identified who your responses refer to, try to be aware that now you are in the presence of God who is Love and not in the presence of your perpetrator. Some self-talk may be helpful, for example, "I am safe! I am not with my perpetrator. I am with God (Jesus) who is Love. God (Jesus) is not my perpetrator or like my perpetrator. God (Jesus) and my perpetrator are very different." 5. Try to silence all the noises in your heart and let God (Jesus) assure you "I am God (Jesus) and I am not your perpetrator!" 6. If you feel calm enough, you may want to proceed with the activity.

[105] The invitation to "touch" Jesus' wounds may stir up traumatic memories associated with the perpetrator. Please refer to footnote #104.

our own wounded history.[106] As you touch Jesus' wounds, notice what is being stirred up in you.

3. At this stage, I would like to invite you to take some time to reflect quietly on your art journal (in chronological order) and the healing journey you have engaged in as you've worked through this handbook.

    Your art journal not only expresses the wounds of your trauma and how you have been impacted but how you have been invited to work through your issues.

    Spend time engaging with each of your drawings, slowly and one by one.

    Each drawing expresses the wounds of your trauma. If you "touch" those wounds again (through remembering how you were when you drew the picture), you may get a surprise to realise that since then, some healing and transformation has taken place within you… Notice if this is the case with each drawing (if not, it is okay! Just because we can't see change, doesn't mean it is not happening).

4. After you have finished reflecting on your drawings, notice how you are feeling (you may be surprised, amazed, encouraged…)

    Are you able to notice and acknowledge some changes and transformation that are happening within you?

    How does this increase your hope to work through the issues of sexual abuse?

5. Take some time now to listen to Jesus saying to you through this Scripture, "Do not doubt but believe!" (You can put your name before the phrase.)

    Try to absorb Jesus' words into your heart.

6. Perhaps after the activity of reflecting on your art journal and "seeing" (noticing) the changes and transformation that have taken place within you, you can believe that the fruit of working through the issues of sexual abuse is healing and transformative.

---

106   Isaiah 53:4a "Surely he has borne our infirmities and carried our diseases…"

In this sense, we can identify with Thomas. Jesus speaks to us with the same words he spoke to Thomas, "Have you believed because you have seen me? Blessed are those who have not seen and yet have come to believe".

Take some time to listen to Jesus saying these words to you.

How are you being invited to live your healing process in the future?

7. You may like to open a new page in your art journal and title it: Believing without seeing.
8. Take some time now to express what you have understood from this activity in a drawing. If it's helpful you may want to draw the scene from Scripture substituting yourself as Thomas.

   Or, you may want to capture in a drawing the changes and transformations that you noticed as you reflected on your art journal while working through this handbook.

Whenever you feel you are losing hope on your healing journey and want to give up, you may find it helpful to re-visit this picture as a reminder to keep moving forward, believing that, through the grace of the risen Jesus, you are changing and transforming even if you do not see it.

The Scripture Experienced in my Life

In order to provide the Department of Public Prosecution with some information that was needed for the trial, I was required to re-visit some geographical locations that were associated with some of my traumatic events.

Prior to this request, I had tried to re-visit some locations associated with my trauma as part of the Exposure Therapy that I was doing with my psychologist.[107] It meant driving through some locations where I'd identify significant objects or places. Automatically, my anxiety levels increased at times to the extent that I would have panic attacks combined with

---

107 Exposure Therapy is a specific type of cognitive-behavioural psychotherapy technique that is often used in the treatment of Post-Traumatic Stress Disorder (PTSD) and phobias. It involves the exposure of the patient to the feared object or context without any danger, in order to overcome their anxiety and/or distress.

distressing flashbacks. Even though it has been nearly three decades since my trauma, the physiological and psychological impacts of it are still so real in my body.

At the particular time that I found myself being triggered, this Scripture reading had immense power to calm me down. Initially, though, I felt like the disciples in the reading who were afraid; my fear related to the fear that overpowered me during my trauma, and for me, the "locked doors" related to my feeling imprisoned and "trapped" which was so real for me during the sexual abuse.

At the time of the trigger, I would visualise the risen Jesus suddenly standing with me in my fear and the sense I had of feeling trapped. Jesus would say to me, "Jane! Peace!" I would cry out in my heart, "Jesus, how can I be peaceful! This is terrifying. I feel like I am going to die!" Jesus would again say, "Jane! Peace!" But again, I would cry out in my heart, "But Jesus, I can't move! I feel paralysed. I feel like I am going to get stuck here!" Again, Jesus would say, "Peace!" And he would keep repeating, "Peace!... Peace!... Peace!... Peace!..." Eventually, I would calm right down.

I recall, though, after several times of exposing myself to possible triggers, I doubted that the exposure therapy was working because I didn't see any immediate benefits. I expressed what I was feeling to my psychologist but I still wanted to give it a fair go, believing in the long run, I would see the fruit of my work.

I was pleasantly surprised on the day I needed to attend one of these locations in order to verify some information for the Department of Public Prosecution. As I was driving to the location, I could feel anxiety arising in me. I brought to mind this Scripture story again, and allowed the Risen Jesus to speak his word, "Peace!"... "Peace in your anxiety!" Jesus kept repeatedly whispering to me, "Peace!" When I arrived at the location, I parked my car in front of the place. I was aware of my fear and my sense of feeling trapped but with a reduced level of emotional intensity compared to previous exposures.

As I sat in my car, I was aware that I was not alone but in the presence of the risen Jesus who offered me, "Peace!" I had a series of flashbacks, as I did previously, only this time I sat calmly with them knowing that Jesus was with me. At the end of each flashback, Jesus invited me to touch his hands, as he did Thomas. I visualised myself doing this and I had the sense that as I touched Jesus' wound, I was touching my own wounded history and the scars of sexual abuse. The pain and despair arising from the flashbacks themselves were evidence of this. Jesus then invited me to touch his side where he had been pierced. I was hesitating to do this because the scar I visualised was large and I was afraid it may still be painful but I found the courage to slowly reach out and touch it. I had a unique spiritual experience in that moment and profound realisation that Jesus' wounded past were interconnected to my wounded past and that his wounds were reflecting my own wounds. As I visualised myself touching his hands and side, I understood at that moment that the risen Jesus completely understood my fear, pain, despair, anxiety and trauma better than anyone else because he experienced it all in his traumatic and tragic death. He could empathise with me better than anyone else.

About fifteen minutes passed and I continued to sit in my car in front of this place that had now become a Sanctuary. Amazingly, I felt so calm. It seemed like my fear, anxiety, despair and the feeling of being trapped had dissolved completely. I acknowledged this as a gift of grace from Jesus. I felt in awe just as I imagine Thomas would have. I sat there saying to Jesus, "There is no one like you on earth! You are powerful. Thank you, Lord!"

I am so grateful for this experience that gave me a new perspective on my healing journey. Yes, I may carry the wounds of a traumatic past but my wounds are being transformed (even though I may not see it at a given time) just as the wounds of the risen Jesus were transformed and changed in the resurrection. Just as life for Jesus was changed and not ended, life for me too did not end with my trauma but it is being and has been changed even to the extent where I, at times, do not recognise the person I am becoming because I am new. I find at these times that I ask myself, "Wait a minute! Can that be right?" I then have a chuckle with Jesus and I say to him, "Well, I believe if it happened to you, it can happen to me!" Jesus chuckles back and says to me, "Don't doubt, Jane, but believe!".

What an extraordinary experience this has been for me! I know that I will certainly be recalling this Scripture everytime I find myself struggling to believe that a new life is possible without seeing it instantaneously.

Your experience of Scripture through prayer, visualisation and art

You may like to take some time to journal about how you have experienced this Scripture reading through art and what it has conveyed to you about your own personal journey. This may be helpful to refer back to in the future.

A New Beginning

OFTEN, IN MY MINISTRY, I have listened to people sharing their belief that the traumas, tragedies and actions of their past define the person they are today. But the truth is that our past can never define who we are. Certainly, we are not our past. We are much more than our past. Even though the impacts of our trauma are experienced in the present, our past is "past"...it has happened... it is gone, in as much as we refer to the context of time. What remains to be lived is our present... the here and now. It is who we choose to be in the present that defines who we are.

This feat doesn't come easily for survivors of sexual abuse because of the false thoughts and beliefs we have put in our mind and heart about who we are. Consequently, we may prevent ourselves from ever reaching our fullest potential and being the best of who we are in our life. We reflect this when we utter things like, "With my history, I will never be able to....", or, "If I wasn't sexually abused in the past, I would be able to...", or, "I am like this now because of my past!" I believe we feel deep sadness in our heart when we limit ourselves by smothering our inner voice of truth that always encourages us to be the best person we can be.

But the good news is that each day brings new opportunities for us to define who we are by being our true self. We don't need to be defined by our traumas of the past, or our circumstances, or things that are out of our control, or other people, or our past behaviours, thoughts or actions. Right now, in the present moment, we can choose to be true to who we are and redefine ourselves by choosing not to: behave with the same behaviours, repeat the same actions, adopt the same attitudes of the past. The more we choose not to be defined by our past, the freer we will become of it and slowly, the best of who we are will begin to emerge.

The key is to know how our past manifests in the present, and to accept how it has shaped us in our thinking, responding, behaving and acting. This empowers us to choose to redefine who we are in the present. For example, because of my thoughts from the past, I keep telling myself, "I am no good! I can't do anything good." These thoughts may be stopping me in the present from attempting to do something that I feel will be good for me and help me to heal and grow. By being aware of my thinking from the past, I can choose in the present to redefine myself by being true to who I am and changing my thoughts to, "I am good and I know that some things I do turn out well". Consequently, I can change my actions and choose to do that certain thing.

We cannot change what has happened to us in our past but we can change our present. The greatest power we have in the present is the power to choose who we want to be. We can use this power to choose growth, to choose change, to choose to transform our life and most of all, to choose to be the best we can be.

The following Scripture account encourages us to believe that our past doesn't define who we are, no matter how traumatic and tragic it has been. Our past is not the end of our story; there is life after trauma and tragedy. This gospel story is very relevant and rich with meaning for our own healing journey. I hope that it leaves you with the keen desire to "Come Forward" and to take hold of the power that you have in the present moment by choosing to be the best of who you are.

The Scripture Reading

Early on the first day of the week, while it was still dark, Mary Magdalene came to the tomb and saw that the stone had been removed from the tomb. So she ran and went to Simon Peter and the other disciple, the one whom Jesus loved, and said to them, "They have taken the Lord out of the tomb, and we do not know where they have laid him." Then Peter and the other disciple set out and went toward the tomb. The two were running together, but the other disciple out ran Peter and reached the tomb first. He bent down to look in and saw the linen wrappings lying there, but he did not go in. Then Simon Peter came, following him, and went into the tomb. He saw the linen wrappings lying there, and the cloth that had been on Jesus' head, not lying with the linen wrappings but rolled up in a place by itself. Then

A New Beginning

the other disciple, who reached the tomb first, also went in, and he saw and believed; for as yet they did not understand the Scripture, that he must rise from the dead. Then the disciples returned to their homes.

But Mary stood weeping outside the tomb. As she wept, she bent over to look into the tomb; and she saw two angels in white, sitting where the body of Jesus had been lying, one at the head and the other at the feet. They said to her, "Woman, why are you weeping?" She said to them, "They have taken away my Lord, and I do not know where they have laid him." When she had said this, she turned around and saw Jesus standing there, but she did not know that it was Jesus. Jesus said to her, "Woman, why are you weeping? Whom are you looking for?" Supposing him to be the gardener, she said to him, "Sir, if you have carried him away, tell me where you have laid him, and I will take him away." Jesus said to her, "Mary!" She turned and said to him in Hebrew, "Rabbouni!" (which means Teacher). Jesus said to her, "Do not hold on to me, because I have not yet ascended to the Father. But go to my brothers and say to them, 'I am ascending to my Father and your Father, to my God and your God.'" Mary Magdalene went and announced to the disciples, "I have seen the Lord"; and she told them that he had said these things to her.

John 20:1-18

This narrative from John describes the event that is at the very heart of our Christian faith. Jesus, who was crucified, has been raised. Trauma, tragedy and death are not the end of Jesus' story, as some of his disciples believed immediately after his death[108] but Jesus' story continues with a new beginning of life after trauma and death.

First of all, we see Mary moving in the darkness of an early morning towards the tomb where Jesus has been laid. When she arrives, the first thing she notices is that the stone in front of the tomb had been removed. Surely, Mary would have been surprised and even troubled. She probably thought, "How can this be? Who's done this! It's impossible for anyone to move this stone on their own! What does this mean?" There are no more details in the story, telling us if

---

108 Luke 24:13-21

Mary enters the tomb or not but she jumps to the conclusion that someone has stolen the body of Jesus, and the message she delivers to Peter and the unnamed disciple is, "They have taken the Lord out of the tomb and we do not know where they have laid him!" Mary is concerned with the body of Jesus; she is concerned with Jesus of the past. She has not yet met him in his risen presence.

We next see Simon Peter and the unnamed disciple arriving to the tomb. Both enter the tomb and see the linen wrappings lying there and the cloth that was on Jesus' head, rolled up and put in a place by itself. The tomb is empty - Jesus' body is not there.

While the "tomb" in this story indicates death, the details noticed by the witnesses communicate life. Both disciples witness that there has been movement inside the tomb; things have shifted and changed. For example: the "stone" at the entrance of the tomb had been miraculously "removed", the linen wrappings that were on the body of Jesus are now lying there in the tomb, curiously, the wrapping previously on Jesus' head is found rolled up in a place on its own, and Jesus' body is not there.

Are these not signs of life within the tomb indicating to us that Jesus is not going to be defined by his past that condemned him to be dead and buried? From within the darkness of the tomb, we are seeing signs of light and the beginnings of a new Creation; signs of Jesus being true to who he is – the Son of God. While in the tomb, he chooses not to be restrained by death, or trauma or tragedy; he chooses to rise above it and to be totally transformed.

It seems that Simon Peter and the unnamed disciple don't really pick up on the grandness of the moment. They go home but there is no rejoicing or celebration yet. Perhaps they are still processing the meaning of the empty tomb.

Mary remains concerned about where the body of Jesus has been laid. She lingers at the tomb distressed. Interestingly, Mary does not experience an empty tomb but there are two angels inside. How significant! The tomb was transformed before her very eyes to a holding place for heavenly life but Mary, in her sadness is oblivious to this and tells the angels of her grief over the missing body of Jesus.

Finally, Mary turns around and sees Jesus but she doesn't recognise him and thinks he is the gardener. He asks her, "Woman, why are you weeping? Who

A New Beginning

are you looking for?" It was a question that went to the core of Mary's grief, "Who was she looking for?"

Up until that point, Mary was looking for Jesus but as she knew him in the past and this prevented her from seeing him alive in the present as a new Creation. (It seems to be that this was also the case with Jesus' disciples who failed to recognise him immediately when he appeared to them.[109]) Mary was witnessing something awesome but she couldn't grasp it; the tragedy of Jesus' past was not the end of his story; rather, it was the beginning of something new and even more magnificent – Life after death.

It is not until Jesus calls Mary by name that she finally recognises him as, "Rabbouni!" (which means "Teacher" in Hebrew). Now, Mary is able to identify Jesus bringing new life and a new creation into being, just as he has done before. Unlike Simon Peter and the unnamed disciple, Mary leaves the garden rejoicing with the certainty that she has seen "the glory as of a Father's only Son, full of grace and truth."[110] For the second time, she runs to the disciples but this time her message is, "I have seen the Lord".

The story of the risen Jesus and Mary's message, "I have seen the Lord", speaks of the new beginning that God has prepared for us all. While the context of this Scripture is referring to the "new beginning" after physical death, it is also relevant in the context of any painful experience that results in spiritual death.

It is a powerful reminder that the traumas and tragedies of our past are not the end of our story and that our past doesn't need to define who we are. It is a story offering us a hope we can bank on; hope for a new beginning in our story – a story of life after trauma and tragedy.

Just as Mary's life was "turned around" when she realised that Jesus was standing there, even though she didn't immediately recognise him, our life will also begin to "turn around" when we recognise the presence of the risen Jesus with us, no matter where we are on our healing journey.

Often, we may find ourselves back in "the tomb", experiencing spiritual death and even though we may feel the grip of darkness; we are invited to believe that we are not alone in our tomb. The risen Jesus is with us even though we may

---

109   Luke 24:15-16; Luke 24:30-31; John 20:19-20; John 21:4; Matthew 28:17
110   John 1:14

not feel his Presence. He understands better than anyone else what it feels like to be in a tomb and he invites us to believe that our tomb will become a holding place for new life and a new beginning just as his did. Like Simon Peter and the unnamed disciple who witnessed the signs of a new beginning within the tomb, we too are invited to witness these signs within ourselves: to notice our "stones" being "removed", or the wrappings of our traumas and tragedies slowly being undone, perhaps other layers of our trauma have been integrated so that we are in a different place, perhaps stuck emotions are gently moving, or past attitudes shifting, or past behaviours and actions changing. It's important to witness the signs of new life and like Mary to leave the tomb rejoicing and celebrating. Celebrating what?

Celebrating that in the presence of the risen Jesus, we have been given the greatest power – the power to rise from our past and not be defined by it, the power to transform and become a new creation; to be the best of ourselves and to live to our fullest potential. Paul, in his letter to the Corinthians, sums up very well the power we have received in the risen Jesus, "everything old has passed away; see, everything has become new!"[111]

May we take hold of the power that has been gifted to us in Jesus Christ so that we may also witness in ourselves "everything old is passing away" and everything is in the process of becoming new.

May this grace of the risen Christ empower us to come forward in our new self and may it bring us a future full of hope and new possibilities.

Experiencing the Scripture through prayer, visualisation and art
(Suggested materials: an A4 or A3 drawing book, crayons, paints or coloured pencils)

1. Take some time to still yourself within and be aware of God's presence with you.
2. Read slowly through the Scripture reading (John 20) and, if you

---

[111] 2 Corinthians 5:17

A New Beginning

are able to, substitute yourself in place of Mary. Try to visualise the scene.

    i) Visualise yourself arriving to the tomb and seeing that the stone in front of it has been removed. Notice the thoughts that are running through your mind.

3. The "tomb" for us may represent the dark place within our self where we experience spiritual death. It is the place where we may often bury ourselves when we feel sad, despairing, fear, confusion, helplessness, loneliness, anger…

    i) On a fresh page in your art journal, you may want to title the page: A New Beginning

    ii) Take some time to visualise your tomb.

    iii) If you had to draw your tomb, what would it look like?

4. Take time now to recognise the signs of life within your tomb:

    i) The "stones" that have been removed (the "stones" can represent the things that have acted as a "block" in your heart). Draw what they look like on your picture.

    ii) The wrappings of our trauma(s) that are being undone. Draw what they look like on your picture.

    iii) The layers of trauma you have worked with and integrated. Draw what they look like on your picture.

    iv) What are the "stuck" emotions that have moved? Draw what they now look like on your picture.

    v) What are your attitudes that have shifted? Try to represent them on your picture.

    vi) What are the behaviours and actions that have changed? Try to represent them on your picture.

5. Mary was unable to recognise that the tomb, once a holding place for the "dead" body of Jesus (Jesus of the past) had been transformed to a holding place of life and the beginning of something new.

    i) Are you able to recognise that your tomb has also

been transformed to a holding place of life where new beginnings are emerging?

6. How is the presence of the risen Jesus evident when you look at your picture? Try to represent the risen Jesus' presence on your drawing.

   The picture you have drawn of your tomb tells a new story – a story of life after trauma. This story is your own story of resurrection and being raised to a new life after the experience of trauma. You may like to write this story out in the section below titled, "Your Experience of Scripture through Art". Just as Jesus' resurrection gifts us with life, hope and courage, so too does your story for others. Perhaps there is someone you know who may be inspired by your story and if you feel comfortable, you may like to share it with them as a means of passing on life, hope and courage.

7. You may like to re-visit your picture in the future and keep adding to it when you recognise certain things are moving, shifting and changing within you. Each time you do, make sure to celebrate the work that God's grace is doing in you through the power of the risen Jesus.

The Scripture Experienced in my Life

At the end of writing this book, I feel like a new beginning is dawning as I emerge from my tomb a new person, thanks to the grace of the risen Jesus.

The writing process has been challenging because it has implied going into "my tomb" (in the context of this chapter) and sitting with my own spiritual darkness so that I could communicate with you from the heart what survivors grapple and deal with on a daily basis.

Although some days have been better than others, every chapter has come with challenges. Had it not been for Christ sharing his power with me - the same power that raised him up from death to life – I do not believe that I could have brought this book to completion. The power of the risen Jesus has been my strength. I have leant heavily on Christ's power to work on each chapter, mentally, spiritually, and emotionally, and I can honestly say that not only has my tomb been transformed but so has my whole being. Thanks to God's grace, I have been made new.

I now know that through the power of the risen Jesus, my tomb is a holding place of new life. During the prayer and writing process, I have felt big "stones" moving. By that, I mean emotions like fear being unblocked; I have unwrapped deeper layers of my shame; I have progressed to integrate other impacts of my trauma; I have noticed my thought processes shifting and some attitudes and behaviours changing. My tomb too is empty. The "I" of my past is not there, for it has been transformed so that all I can see is the "I" that I am now. I am left in awe at the power of the risen Jesus.

I feel gifted by grace, to savour and taste something of what Christ must have felt as he walked out of the tomb and came forward into new life and a new beginning! What joy! What glory! What a feeling of triumph! I feel that for me this is the beginning of a new story – a story of Life after Trauma and I am truly grateful for this New Beginning.

Your experience of Scripture through prayer, visualisation and art

You may like to take some time to journal about how you have experienced this Scripture reading through art and what it has conveyed to you about your own personal journey. This may be helpful to refer back to in the future.

"Everything old has passed away; see, everything has become new!"

2 Corinthians 5:17

Appendix 1

A blueprint for praying with the Bible
(Word of God/the Scriptures)

Prayer is a dialogue with God

We speak to God

Awareness & acknowledgment of God's Presence with us (As if you were meeting a friend, *"Hello, God! It's good to be here with you. How are you?"*)

God speaks to us

We listen to God through a specific reading from the Bible (Word of God/Scriptures)

How? See "Listening to God through a Specific Reading" page 192.

We speak to God

Always **conclude** prayer with a *resolution* (Remember that God invites us not only to listen to his Word but to practise and translate it in our life).

Is there something God is inviting me to do differently or change in my life so that it is more fruitful?

Through our Baptism, Christ invites us all to participate in his Mission by sharing the Good News with others.

Who is God inviting me to share this prayer with?
How will I share it (through a Word, an action, a different attitude)?

Listening to God through a specific reading

1. Before you take up the Scripture reading, try to be aware that it is God who is about to speak to you through these words.
2. Read the specific Scripture reading very slowly, aware of each word and, as you do, try to make the reading as personal as possible by substituting your name where "you" is mentioned or where a character comes into play (for example if it talks about the "blind man", the "Samaritan Woman", or "Zacchaeus", substitute your name instead). If you are able to, try to visualise the scene.
3. Once you have read it slowly, following the steps above, go back to the words or phrase(s) that have called your attention in some way (it may be that they evoked a feeling in you: joy, wonder, surprise, sadness, fear, hope, encouragement). This is important because God wants to speak to you personally through these words.
4. Try to begin a dialogue with God around these specific words expressing to him whatever thoughts may come to mind, or feelings that are aroused, or questions that arise from them. (For example, why do you say that, God? Or why did you do that? Or those words cause me to feel afraid, are they meant to, God?) Try to listen to God's response in your heart.
5. Try to have a deeper dialogue with God around the topic of the specific Scripture that you are reading (It may be around his compassion, forgiveness, unconditional love…). Remember, once you have expressed yourself to God, keep trying to listen to his response through his Word. Do not be rushed to move on but try to savour God's words through Scripture as much as you can.
6. When you feel that nothing more is happening, then move on to the next part of the Scripture reading that calls your attention, repeating the steps above.
7. When you have finished listening to God through the Scripture reading, try to conclude your session of prayer by making a resolution.

Appendix 2

Support Services

Australian Childhood Trauma Group
Professional support.
website www.theactgroup.com.au/ *phone* (03) 9415 6066

Blue Knot Foundation (Previously known as Adults Surviving Child Abuse – ASCA)
National professional phone counselling, information and support for adult survivors of child abuse with referral database of experienced professionals and agencies 9-5 EST, 7 days. Workshops for survivors, workshops for family members, partners and friends.
website www.blueknot.org.au *phone* 1300 657 380 *email* helpline@blueknot.org.au

Bravehearts
Specialist case management, counselling and telephone counselling for child and adult survivors, non-offending family members and friends.
website: www.bravehearts.org.au *phone* 1800 272 831 (7am – 8pm AEST Time) *email* rc@bravehearts.org.au

Care Leavers Australia Network
Support and advocacy for people who grew up in Australian orphanages, childrens homes and in foster care, and their families. Counselling and case management available.
website www.clan.org.au *phone* 1800 008 774 *email* support@clan.org.auh

Child Migrants Trust
Social work services including counselling and support for family reunions.
website www.childmigrantstrust.com *phone* 1800 040 509

Child Wise
Trauma informed telephone and online counselling for childhood abuse. Training and organisational capacity building on child abuse prevention.
website www.childwise.net *phone* 1800 99 10 99

Children with Disability Australia
Provides information, referrals and education to people with disabilities.
website www.cda.org.au *phone* 1800 222 660

CREATE Foundation
Information, support and advocacy for young people up to 25 years of age.
website www.create.org.au *phone* 1800 655 105

Drummond St Services Vic
Provides a wide range of support and recovery for individuals, families, couples, young people and children.
website www.ds.org.au/ *phone* (03) 9663 6733

Find and Connect
Support and counselling for Forgotten Australians and former Child Migrants, Family tracing and access to care records.
website www.findandconnect.gov.au phone 1800 161 109

Headspace
Counselling and referral service for young people aged 12-25 years. Also supports parents.
website www.headspace.org.au *phone* 1800 650 890
online counselling www.eheadspace.org.au

Healing Foundation
Service to help build the capacity of Indigenous organisations and support the development of the Link Up network.
website healingfoundation.org.au *phone* (02) 6124 4400 (NSW)

Heartfelt House, Alstonville, Northern Rivers Region
Support to adult survivors of childhood sexual abuse and their family and friends by qualified counsellors
website www.heartfelthouse.org.au *phone* 02 6628 8940
email heartfelthouse@westnet.com.au

In Good Faith and Associates
Provides counselling and support services to people who have experienced religious/clergy abuse.
website www.igfa.com.au *phone* (03) 9326 5991

Interrelate
Counselling and support for those affected by institutional Child Sexual Abuse and Royal Commission. Locations: Dubbo, Caringbah, Bella-Vista, Muswellbrook, Port Macquarie, Coffs Harbour and Lismore (and other).
website www.interrelate.org.au *phone* 1300 13 49 24 (Mon-Fri; 9-5pm)
email RCCBSS@interrelate.org.au

Support Services

Laurel House North and North West
Therapeutic services and support for men, women and children impacted by sexual violence
website www.laurelhouse.org.au *phone* 03 6334 2740
24/7 counselling phone 03 6431 9711 *email* counsellors@laurelhouse.org.au

Lifeline
24-hour crisis support and suicide prevention.
website www.lifeline.org.au *phone* 13 11 14

Lighthouse Foundation
Specialist attachment and trauma informed training
website www.lighthousefoundation.org.au *phone* 03 9093 7500

Link Up NSW Aboriginal Corporation
Provides counselling, healing and culturally appropriate support for indigenous Australians.
website www.linkupnsw.org.au *phone* 1800 624 332

MensLine Australia
A national telephone and online support, information and referral service for men with family and relationship concerns.
website www.mensline.org.au *phone* 1300 78 99 78 (available 24/7)
online counselling www.mensline.org.au

NSW Rape Crisis Centre
Crisis counselling service for anyone in Australia who has experienced or is at risk of sexual assault - staffed by qualified trauma counsellors.
website www.nswrapecrisis.com.au/ *phone* 1800 424 017

People with Disability Australia
Operating a national telephone line for advice, information, referrals and advocacy support. Provides training and individual advocacy support to people with disability.
website www.pwd.org.au *phone* 1800 422 015 *TTY number* 1800 422 016

Rape and Domestic Violence Services Australia
27/7 telephone and online crisis counselling, information and referral for anyone in NSW who has experienced or is at risk of sexual assault. Staffed by trauma specialist counsellors.
websites www.rap-dservices.org.au www.nswrapecrisis.com.au
phone 1800 424 017 (24/7)

Relationships Australia NSW
Individual and family counselling. Intake and referral to additional specialist support services for people affected by the Royal Commission
website www.nsw.relationships.com.au *phone* 1800 025 441 (Mon - Fri 9am - 5pm)
email (Mon - Fri 9am - 5pm) royalcommissioncommunitybasedsupport@ransw.org.au

Relationships Australia Tasmania
Family and relationship counselling and specialist support services for individuals affected by the Royal Commission. Offices located at Devonport, Launceston and Hobart.
website www.tas.relationships.org.au/ *phone* 1300 364 277

Relationships Australia
Family and relationship counselling as well as a range of specialist counselling services.
website www.relationships.org.au *phone* 1800 025 441
email (Mon - Fri 9am - 5pm) royalcommissioncommunitybasedsupport@ransw.org.au

Sexual Assault Support Services – NSW Health
Information, counselling, court support for anyone who has been sexually assaulted in NSW
website www.sexualassaultcounselling.org.au *phone* 1800 211 028

Sexual Assault Support Services Inc
Counselling and support for men, women affected by sexual assault, survivors of sexual abuse, family members and support people.
website www.sass.org.au/ *phone* (03) 6231 1817 *email* admin@sass.org.au

Suicide Call Back Service
24/7 counselling for people 18 years and over who are suicidal, caring for someone who is suicidal or people bereaved by suicide.
website pwww.suicidecallbackservice.org.auphone 1300 659 467

Survivors and Mates Support Network (SAMSN)
Facilitated groups and workshops for male survivors of childhood sexual abuse and their families.
website www.samsn.com.au *phone* 0439 838 787 *email* support@samsn.com.au

Tzedek
Provides advocacy, referrals and support services to people who have experienced religious/clergy abuse, with a focus on the Jewish community.
website www.tzedek.org.au *phone* 1300 893 335 *email* info@tzedek.org.au

Support Services

Victims Access Line
Single entry point for Victims of Crime in NSW to assist them in accessing services, including counselling and support.
website www.lawlink.nsw.gove.au/vs *phone* 1800 633 063 *email* vs@agd.nsw.gov.au
Aboriginal contact line 1800 019 123

Victims Support Services
Personal support, counselling, information and referral services to help people deal with the impact of crime.
website www.justice.tas.gov.au *24 hour counselling* 1 300 300 238
email victims@justice.tas.gov.au

Victorian Centres against Sexual Assault
Provide free ongoing specialist counselling and support for victim/survivors and family members of those who have experienced sexual assault, including those affected by institutional abuse.
website www.casa.org.au *phone* 1800 806 292 (24/7)

The Women's Cottage, Hawkesbury
Community based support and resource centre run by women, for women and children.
phone (02) 4578 4190

1800 Respect
24/7 telephone and online crisis counselling, information and referral for anyone in Australia who has experienced or been impacted by sexual assault, domestic or family violence. Staffed by trauma specialist counsellors.
website www.1800respect.org.au *phone* 1 800 737 732
online counselling www.1800respect.org.au

www.ingramcontent.com/pod-product-compliance
Lightning Source LLC
Chambersburg PA
CBHW070254010526
44107CB00056B/2452